AF765683

Mastering USS Made Simple: A Practical Guide to Modernizing Your Mainframe Without Linux Expertise

Mainframes

Ricardo Nuqui

Published by Isaac Nangan, 2025.

While every precaution has been taken in the preparation of this book, the publisher assumes no responsibility for errors or omissions, or for damages resulting from the use of the information contained herein.

MASTERING USS MADE SIMPLE: A PRACTICAL GUIDE TO MODERNIZING YOUR MAINFRAME WITHOUT LINUX EXPERTISE

First edition. May 27, 2025.

Copyright © 2025 Ricardo Nuqui.

ISBN: 979-8231764044

Written by Ricardo Nuqui.

Table of Contents

TO COLEEN, SKY AND NEO. YOU ARE MY INSPIRATIONS.

MASTERING
USS MADE
SIMPLE
A PRACTICAL GUIDE TO
MODERNIZING YOUR MAINFRAME
WITHOUT LINUX EXPERTISE

Mastering USS Made Simple: A Practical Guide to Modernizing Your Mainframe Without Linux Expertise

Ricardo Nuqui

Preface

Welcome to "Mastering USS Made Simple: A Practical Guide to Modernizing Your Mainframe Without Linux Expertise."

In today's rapidly evolving IT landscape, organizations are under constant pressure to modernize their systems while maintaining reliability, security, and efficiency. For many businesses, the mainframe remains a cornerstone of their operations—powerful, dependable, and capable of handling massive workloads. However, modernization is no longer optional; it's essential for staying competitive and meeting the demands of a digital-first world.

This book was born out of a simple yet powerful idea: you don't need to be a Linux expert to harness the full potential of z/OS UNIX System Services (USS). Whether you're an IT professional new to the mainframe world or a seasoned operator looking to modernize workflows, this guide will equip you with the knowledge and tools to leverage USS effectively. By focusing on practical, real-world applications, we aim to demystify USS and empower you to drive meaningful change within your organization.

Why This Book?

Mainframe modernization can feel daunting, especially when faced with complex technologies and unfamiliar terminology. Many resources assume a deep understanding of Linux or advanced scripting skills, leaving beginners overwhelmed. This book bridges that gap by breaking down concepts into easy-to-understand language and providing step-by-step instructions.

We've structured the content to align with both the online course and real-world application. Each chapter builds on the previous one, ensuring a logical progression from foundational knowledge to advanced techniques. Along the way, you'll find real-world examples, hands-on exercises, and troubleshooting tips designed to reinforce your learning and prepare you for challenges in the field.

Who Is This Book For?

This book is written for:

- IT Professionals: Those responsible for managing or modernizing mainframe environments who want to expand their skill set without diving into full Linux expertise.
- System Administrators: Individuals tasked with optimizing workflows, automating tasks, and improving system performance using USS.
- Business Leaders: Managers and decision-makers seeking to understand how USS can align with organizational goals and deliver measurable value.
- Learners at All Levels: Whether you're just starting your journey with USS or looking to refine your skills, this book offers something for everyone.

How to Use This Book

This book is designed to be flexible. You can read it cover-to-cover as a comprehensive guide or use it as a reference to tackle specific challenges. If you're following along with the online course, each chapter corresponds to key lessons, providing additional context and insights. If you're applying what you've learned in the real world, the practical examples and best practices will serve as a valuable resource.

What Sets This Book Apart?

While the online course provides a structured learning path, this book dives deeper into topics due to the lack of time constraints. You'll find expanded explanations, advanced techniques, and real-world case studies that go beyond the scope of the course. Additionally, we've included sections on integrating USS with other technologies, optimizing performance, and addressing security considerations—topics that are critical for long-term success but may not fit into a 30-minute lesson.

A Note of Encouragement

Modernizing your mainframe environment is a journey, not a destination. It requires patience, persistence, and a willingness to learn. But with the right tools and guidance, you can transform your workflows, reduce costs, and position your organization for future growth.

By the time you finish this book, you'll have a solid understanding of USS and the confidence to apply it in real-world scenarios. More importantly, you'll be equipped to lead modernization initiatives that deliver tangible business value.

So, let's get started. The future of your mainframe—and your career—awaits.

Happy learning,

Ricardo Nuqui

Author

Prologue: The Case for Modernizing Your Mainframe

The mainframe has long been the backbone of enterprise IT systems, powering mission-critical applications for industries such as banking, healthcare, retail, and government. Known for its reliability, scalability, and security, the mainframe remains an indispensable asset for organizations that demand high performance and zero downtime. Yet, despite its strengths, the mainframe often faces criticism for being outdated or difficult to integrate with modern technologies.

This perception is not entirely unfounded. Many organizations struggle to modernize their mainframe environments due to a lack of expertise, resources, or clear strategies. The result? Legacy workflows that are inefficient, error-prone, and costly to maintain. But here's the good news: modernization doesn't require replacing your mainframe—it requires reimagining how you use it.

Enter z/OS UNIX System Services (USS) , a powerful yet underutilized tool that bridges the gap between traditional mainframe operations and modern computing practices. USS allows you to automate repetitive tasks, streamline workflows, and integrate seamlessly with non-mainframe environments—all without requiring full Linux expertise. It's the key to unlocking the untapped potential of your mainframe while aligning with today's business needs.

Why Now Is the Time to Act

The pressure to modernize has never been greater. Customers expect faster service, employees demand more efficient tools, and executives seek ways to reduce costs without sacrificing quality. At the same time, emerging technologies like cloud computing, artificial intelligence, and big data analytics are transforming how businesses operate. Organizations that fail to adapt risk falling behind their competitors.

Modernizing your mainframe with USS isn't just about keeping up—it's about staying ahead. By automating manual processes, improving system performance, and enabling cross-platform integration, USS empowers you to:

- Reduce Operational Costs: Automate routine tasks to minimize labor-intensive efforts and eliminate errors.
- Improve Efficiency: Streamline workflows to reduce processing times and improve throughput.
- Enhance Scalability: Build flexible solutions that grow with your organization's needs.
- Drive Business Value: Align technical initiatives with strategic goals like cost reduction, innovation, and customer satisfaction.

A Story of Transformation

Consider the story of a large financial institution struggling with nightly batch processing. Each night, hundreds of datasets had to be processed manually, leading to delays, errors, and skyrocketing overtime costs. Frustrated by inefficiencies, the IT team decided to explore USS as a solution.

By automating these tasks with USS scripts, they reduced processing times by 40%, eliminated manual intervention errors, and saved tens of thousands of dollars annually in labor costs. More importantly, they demonstrated measurable value to leadership, securing approval to expand USS adoption across the organization. What started as a small initiative became a catalyst for broader modernization efforts.

This story isn't unique—it's representative of what's possible when you embrace USS as a tool for change. Whether you're automating file transfers, integrating with cloud platforms, or optimizing resource utilization, USS can help you achieve your modernization goals.

Your Role in the Journey

As someone committed to mastering USS, you play a vital role in this transformation. You're not just learning a new skill—you're positioning yourself as a leader in your organization's modernization journey. The knowledge you gain from this book will enable you to:

- Solve real-world challenges with practical, actionable solutions.
- Communicate the value of USS to stakeholders and secure their buy-in.
- Lead pilot projects and scale successful initiatives across teams.

But remember, modernization is not a solo endeavor. It requires collaboration, creativity, and a willingness to experiment. Along the way, you'll encounter obstacles—but you'll also discover opportunities to innovate and make a lasting impact.

What Lies Ahead

In the chapters that follow, we'll take you step-by-step through everything you need to know about USS. From foundational concepts to advanced techniques, each chapter builds on the last, ensuring you develop a comprehensive understanding of how to leverage USS effectively. We'll also share real-world examples, troubleshooting tips, and best practices to guide you through common challenges.

Whether you're reading this book alongside the online course or using it as a standalone resource, our goal is simple: to empower you with the knowledge and confidence to modernize your mainframe environment successfully.

So, let's embark on this journey together. The tools, strategies, and insights you'll gain from this book will not only transform your mainframe but also elevate your career.

Let's get started.

Introduction

Chapter 1. Welcome to the World of USS

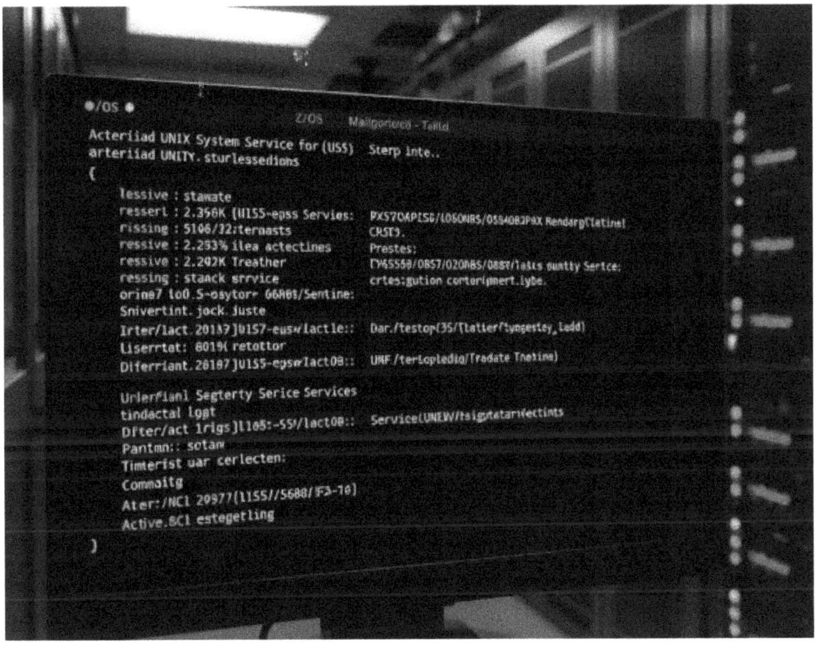

What is USS and Why Does It Matter?

z/OS UNIX System Services (USS) is a robust component of IBM's z/OS operating system that brings UNIX-like functionality to the mainframe environment. It provides a familiar interface for users accustomed to UNIX or Linux systems while maintaining the reliability, security, and scalability of the mainframe.

USS matters because it bridges the gap between traditional mainframe operations and modern computing practices. Whether you're automating repetitive tasks, integrating with cloud platforms, or streamlining workflows, USS offers tools and capabilities that make these processes faster, more efficient, and less error-prone. In short, USS empowers you to modernize your mainframe without requiring full Linux expertise.

The Role of USS in Modernization

Modernization isn't about replacing your mainframe—it's about maximizing its potential. USS plays a pivotal role in this effort by enabling automation, cross-platform integration, and resource optimization. For example:

- Automating nightly batch jobs reduces manual effort and errors.
- Integrating USS with JCL workflows ensures compatibility and efficiency.
- Leveraging scripting languages like Python or shell scripts enhances flexibility and innovation.

By adopting USS, organizations can achieve measurable improvements in efficiency, cost savings, and scalability—key drivers of successful modernization initiatives.

Who This Book Is For

This book is designed for anyone looking to harness the power of USS, regardless of their experience level. If you're new to the mainframe world, this guide will introduce you to USS concepts in an accessible way. If you're already familiar with z/OS but want to deepen your understanding of USS, you'll find advanced techniques and real-world examples to expand your skills.

How to Use This Book

This book is structured to support both sequential learning and targeted reference. Beginners can read it from start to finish to build a solid foundation, while experienced users can jump directly to specific chapters for guidance on particular topics. Each section includes practical examples, troubleshooting tips, and actionable insights to help you apply what you've learned in real-world scenarios.

Chapter 2. Getting Started with USS

Understanding z/OS UNIX System Services (USS)

At its core, USS is a subsystem within z/OS that provides a UNIX-like environment for running scripts, managing files, and executing commands. It supports hierarchical file systems, multi-tasking, and standard utilities like **ls**, **cp**, and **grep**. Unlike traditional mainframe environments, USS allows you to work with familiar UNIX tools while leveraging the strengths of z/OS.

Key features of USS include:

- Hierarchical File System: Organizes files and directories in a tree-like structure.

- Shell Environment: Provides a command-line interface for executing scripts and utilities.
- Cross-Platform Compatibility: Enables integration with non-mainframe systems and technologies.

Navigating the USS Environment

To get started, you'll need to access the USS environment through a terminal or emulator. Once logged in, you can use basic commands to navigate directories and manage files. Here are some essential commands:

- **cd**: Change directories.
- **ls**: List files and directories.
- **pwd**: Display the current working directory.

These commands form the foundation of your interaction with USS and will become second nature as you gain experience.

Key Concepts: Files, Directories, and Permissions

Understanding how files and directories work in USS is crucial for effective system management.

- Files: Data stored in the USS environment, similar to files in a UNIX or Linux system.
- Directories: Containers that organize files into a hierarchical structure.
- Permissions: Controls who can read, write, or execute files and directories.

Permissions are particularly important for maintaining security and ensuring proper access. You'll learn how to manage permissions using commands like **chmod** and **chown** later in this book.

Setting Up Your First USS Workflow

A practical way to get hands-on experience with USS is to set up a simple workflow. For example, you might create a script to automate the copying of files from one directory to another. Here's how you can do it:

1. Open your terminal and navigate to the desired directory using **cd**.
2. Create a new file using a text editor like **vi** or **nano**.
3. Write a basic script, such as:

```
#!/bin/sh
cp /path/to/source/file /path/to/destination/
```

1. Save the file and make it executable with **chmod +x filename.sh**.
2. Run the script using **./filename.sh**.

This simple exercise introduces you to the basics of USS scripting and sets the stage for more complex workflows as you progress.

With these foundational concepts in place, you're ready to dive deeper into the world of USS. The next chapters will guide you through advanced scripting, troubleshooting, and strategies for aligning USS with organizational goals. Let's continue building your expertise—one step at a time.

Part 1: Foundations of USS

Welcome to Part 1: Foundations of USS , where we lay the groundwork for mastering z/OS UNIX System Services (USS). This section is designed to equip you with the essential skills and knowledge needed to navigate, manage, and automate tasks within the USS environment. Whether you're new to USS or looking to refine your understanding, this part will provide a solid foundation upon which you can build more advanced capabilities.

Why Start with the Foundations?

Before you can effectively modernize workflows or lead large-scale initiatives, you need to understand the core tools and techniques that make USS so powerful. These foundational skills will not only help you perform everyday tasks but also prepare you for more complex challenges down the road. Think of this section as your toolkit—a collection of commands, scripts, and troubleshooting strategies that you'll use repeatedly in real-world scenarios.

What You'll Learn in This Part

This section is divided into three key chapters, each focusing on a critical aspect of working with USS:

1. Introduction to USS Commands
   In this chapter, you'll learn the fundamental commands that allow you to interact with the USS environment. From navigating directories (**cd**, **ls**, **pwd**) to managing files (**cp**, **mv**, **rm**) and permissions (**chmod**, **chown**), these tools are the building blocks of any USS workflow. Mastery of these

commands will give you the confidence to manage your mainframe environment efficiently.

2. Automating Tasks with Shell Scripts
   Automation is at the heart of modernization, and shell scripting is one of the most effective ways to achieve it. This chapter introduces you to the basics of writing shell scripts, including how to use variables, loops, and conditionals to create dynamic and reusable solutions. You'll also explore debugging techniques with **set -x** and see real-world examples of how automation can streamline repetitive tasks and improve productivity.
3. Monitoring and Troubleshooting USS Workflows
   Even the best-designed workflows can encounter issues, so monitoring and troubleshooting are essential skills. This chapter covers how to use logs for proactive monitoring, leverage tools like **tail -f** for live updates, and extract actionable insights with **grep** and **awk**. You'll also learn how to identify and resolve common errors, ensuring your USS implementations run smoothly and reliably.

How This Part Fits Into the Bigger Picture

The skills you gain in this section will serve as the backbone of your USS expertise. Understanding basic commands and file management prepares you to tackle more advanced topics, such as integrating USS with other technologies or scaling automation across teams. Similarly, learning how to monitor and troubleshoot workflows ensures that you can address challenges as they arise, making you a more effective problem-solver and leader.

By the end of this part, you'll have a comprehensive understanding of the foundational tools and techniques that make USS a powerful ally in modernizing your mainframe environment. With these skills in hand, you'll be ready to move on to more advanced topics, such as aligning USS with business goals and executing pilot projects.

Let's dive in and start building your USS expertise—one command, script, and log entry at a time.

Chapter 3. Introduction to USS Commands

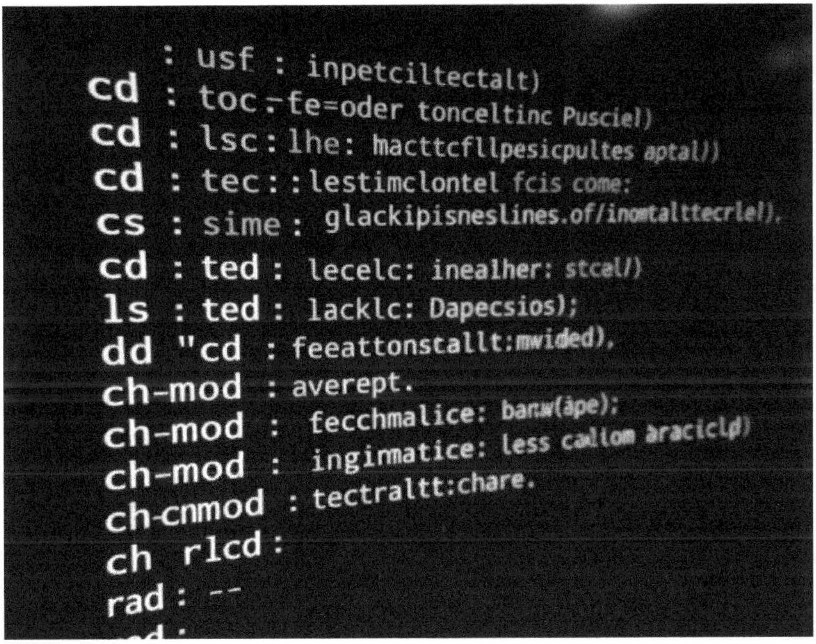

The power of z/OS UNIX System Services (USS) lies in its ability to provide a familiar, command-driven environment for managing files, directories, and workflows. In this chapter, we'll explore the foundational commands that allow you to navigate, manage, and secure your USS environment effectively. These commands are the building blocks of any USS workflow, and mastering them is essential for success.

Basic Navigation Commands (cd, ls, pwd)

Before you can manage files or automate tasks, you need to know how to move around the USS environment. The following navigation commands will help you locate and organize your work efficiently.

1. **cd** (Change Directory):
   The **cd** command allows you to change your current working directory. Think of it as moving from one folder to another in a graphical file explorer.
    - Example:

cd /u/user/documents
This command moves you to the **/u/user/documents** directory.

- Use **cd ..** to move up one directory level or **cd ~** to return to your home directory.

1. **ls** (List Files and Directories):
   The **ls** command displays the contents of a directory, helping you see what files and subdirectories are available.
    - Example:

ls -l

The **-l** option provides a detailed listing, including file permissions, ownership, size, and modification date.

- Other useful options:
    - **ls -a**: Shows hidden files (those starting with a dot).
    - **ls -R**: Recursively lists all files in subdirectories.

1. **pwd** (Print Working Directory):
   The **pwd** command tells you your current location within the directory structure. This is especially helpful when navigating

complex hierarchies.

- Example:

pwd
Output:
/u/user/projects

By mastering these navigation commands, you'll be able to move confidently through the USS environment and locate the resources you need.

File Management Commands (cp, mv, rm)

Once you're comfortable navigating, the next step is learning how to manage files and directories. These commands allow you to copy, move, rename, and delete files—essential tasks for organizing and maintaining your USS workflows.

1. **cp** (Copy):
   The **cp** command creates a copy of a file or directory.
   - Example:

cp file1.txt file2.txt
This copies **file1.txt** to a new file named **file2.txt**.

- To copy directories, use the **-r** (recursive) option:

cp -r dir1 dir2
This copies the entire **dir1** directory and its contents to **dir2**.

1. **mv** (Move/Rename):
   The **mv** command moves or renames files and directories.
   - Example (Renaming):

mv oldname.txt newname.txt

This renames **oldname.txt** to **newname.txt**.

- Example (Moving):

mv file.txt /u/user/archive/
This moves **file.txt** to the /**u**/**user**/**archive**/ directory.

1. **rm** (Remove):
   The **rm** command deletes files or directories. Be cautious when using this command, as deleted files cannot be recovered.
      - Example:

rm file.txt
This deletes **file.txt**.

- To remove directories, use the **-r** option:

rm -r dir1

This deletes the **dir1** directory and all its contents.

These file management commands are indispensable for keeping your USS environment organized and efficient. Practice them regularly to build confidence and avoid accidental deletions.

Working with Permissions (chmod, chown)

Permissions are a critical aspect of file and directory management in USS. Properly setting permissions ensures that only authorized users can access, modify, or execute files. Let's explore the two primary commands for managing permissions: **chmod** and **chown**.

1. **chmod** (Change Mode):
   The **chmod** command modifies file or directory permissions. Permissions are divided into three categories:

- Read (**r**): Allows viewing the file's contents.
- Write (**w**): Allows modifying or deleting the file.
- Execute (**x**): Allows running the file as a script or program.

Permissions can be set for three groups of users:

- Owner: The user who owns the file.
- Group: Users who belong to the file's group.
- Others: Everyone else.
- Example:

chmod 755 script.sh
This sets the following permissions:

- Owner: Read, write, and execute (7).
- Group: Read and execute (**5**).
- Others: Read and execute (**5**).

Alternatively, you can use symbolic notation:
chmod u+x script.sh
This adds execute permission for the owner (**u**).

1. **chown** (Change Ownership):
   The **chown** command changes the owner or group of a file or directory.
   - Example:

chown user1 file.txt
This changes the owner of **file.txt** to **user1**.

- To change both owner and group:

chown user1:group1 file.txt

1. Properly managing ownership ensures accountability and security, particularly in multi-user environments.

Why These Commands Matter

The commands covered in this chapter—navigation, file management, and permissions—are the foundation of every USS workflow. They enable you to:

- Organize and maintain your environment efficiently.
- Automate repetitive tasks with precision.
- Secure sensitive data through proper permissions.

As you progress through this book, you'll find yourself returning to these commands repeatedly. They are the tools that empower you to take control of your USS environment and drive meaningful modernization efforts.

With these foundational skills in hand, you're now ready to move on to more advanced topics, such as automating tasks with shell scripts and monitoring workflows. Keep practicing these commands—they're the cornerstone of your USS expertise!

Chapter 4. Automating Tasks with Shell Scripts

Automation is at the heart of modernization, and shell scripting is one of the most powerful tools for achieving it within z/OS UNIX System Services (USS). By writing scripts, you can streamline repetitive tasks, reduce manual errors, and improve efficiency. In this chapter, we'll walk through the process of creating your first shell script, explore advanced scripting techniques like variables, loops, and conditionals, and learn how to debug and refine your scripts. Finally, we'll look at real-world examples of automation to inspire your own projects.

Writing Your First Shell Script

A shell script is essentially a text file containing a series of commands that the system executes sequentially. Writing your first script is straightforward, and it's a great way to get hands-on experience with USS automation.

1. Create a New Script File:
   Start by creating a new file using a text editor like **vi** or **nano.**
   For example:

```
vi myscript.sh
```

1. Add a Shebang Line:
   The first line of your script should specify the interpreter to use. For most shell scripts, this will be **#!/bin/sh**:

```
#!/bin/sh
```

1. Write Commands:
   Add the commands you want the script to execute. For example, here's a simple script that lists files in a directory:

```
#!/bin/sh
echo "Listing files in the current directory:"
ls -l
```

1. Save and Exit:
   Save the file and exit the editor.
2. Make the Script Executable:
   Use the **chmod** command to make the script executable:

```
chmod +x myscript.sh
```

1. Run the Script:
   Execute the script by typing:

```
./myscript.sh
```

Congratulations! You've just written and executed your first shell script. This basic framework can be expanded to handle more complex tasks as you grow your skills.

Using Variables, Loops, and Conditionals

To create dynamic and reusable scripts, you'll need to incorporate variables, loops, and conditionals. These elements allow your scripts to adapt to different inputs and scenarios.

1. Variables:
   Variables store values that can be reused throughout your script. For example:

```
#!/bin/sh
NAME="John"
echo "Hello, $NAME!"
```

Output:

```
Hello, John!
```

You can also capture user input using the **read** command:

```
#!/bin/sh
echo "What is your name?"
read NAME
echo "Hello, $NAME!"
```

1. Loops:
   Loops allow you to repeat a set of commands multiple times. There are two common types of loops: **for** and **while**.

- For Loop:

```
#!/bin/sh
for FILE in *.txt
do
echo "Processing $FILE"
done
```

This script processes all **.txt** files in the current directory.

- While Loop:

```
#!/bin/sh
COUNT=1
while [ $COUNT -le 5 ]
do
echo "Count: $COUNT"
COUNT=$((COUNT + 1))
done
```

This script counts from 1 to 5.

1. Conditionals:
   Conditionals allow your script to make decisions based on specific criteria. The **if** statement is the most common conditional structure.

```
#!/bin/sh
NUM=10
if [ $NUM -gt 5 ]
then
echo "$NUM is greater than 5."
else
echo "$NUM is 5 or less."
fi
```

Output:
10 is greater than 5.

By combining variables, loops, and conditionals, you can create highly flexible and powerful scripts tailored to your organization's needs.

Debugging Scripts with set -x

Even the best-written scripts can encounter issues, so knowing how to debug them is essential. One of the simplest and most effective debugging tools is the **set -x** command, which enables tracing mode. When **set -x** is enabled, the shell prints each command and its arguments as they are executed, helping you identify where things might be going wrong.

1. Enable Debugging:
   Add **set -x** at the beginning of your script or before the section you want to debug. For example:

```
#!/bin/sh
set -x
echo "Starting script..."
ls -l
echo "Script complete."
```

1. Disable Debugging:
   Use **set +x** to turn off tracing mode when you no longer need it. For example:

```
#!/bin/sh
set -x
echo "This part will be traced."
set +x
echo "This part will not be traced."
```

Debugging with **set -x** is an invaluable skill that will save you time and frustration as you develop more complex scripts.

Real-World Examples of Automation

Now that you've learned the basics of shell scripting, let's explore some practical examples of how USS automation can solve real-world challenges.

1. Automating File Backups:
   A common task in IT is backing up files regularly. Here's a script that copies files to a backup directory and logs the operation:

```
#!/bin/sh
BACKUP_DIR="/u/user/backups"
LOG_FILE="/u/user/logs/backup.log"
echo "Backup started at $(date)" >> $LOG_FILE
cp -r /u/user/data/* $BACKUP_DIR
echo "Backup completed at $(date)" >> $LOG_FILE
```

1. Monitoring Disk Usage:
   Monitoring disk usage helps prevent storage-related issues. This script checks disk usage and sends an alert if it exceeds a threshold:

```
#!/bin/sh

THRESHOLD=80

USAGE=$(df -h | grep '/dev/' | awk '{print $5}' | sed
's/%//g')

if [ $USAGE -gt $THRESHOLD ]

then
```

```
echo "Warning: Disk usage is above ${THRESHOLD}%." | mail -s "Disk Usage Alert" admin@example.com

fi
```

1. Processing Batch Files:
   Automating nightly batch jobs is a classic use case for USS. This script processes all **.dat** files in a directory:

```
#!/bin/sh
for FILE in /u/user/input/*.dat
do
echo "Processing $FILE..."
# Replace this with your processing logic
mv $FILE /u/user/archive/
done
echo "All files processed."
```

These examples demonstrate how shell scripts can simplify and enhance routine tasks, freeing up time for more strategic initiatives.

Why Automation Matters

Automation is more than just a convenience—it's a necessity for modern organizations. By automating repetitive tasks, you can:

- Reduce manual effort and human error.
- Improve consistency and reliability.
- Free up resources to focus on higher-value activities.

As you gain confidence with shell scripting, you'll find countless opportunities to apply these skills in your daily work. Whether it's streamlining workflows, integrating systems, or optimizing resource utilization, automation with USS is a game-changer.

With these scripting fundamentals under your belt, you're well-equipped to tackle more advanced topics, such as monitoring and troubleshooting USS workflows. Keep experimenting and refining your scripts—they're the key to unlocking the full potential of USS!

Chapter 5. Monitoring and Troubleshooting USS Workflows

Monitoring and troubleshooting are critical skills for ensuring the reliability, efficiency, and performance of your USS workflows. In this chapter, we'll explore how to use logs for proactive monitoring, leverage tools like **tail -f** for real-time updates, extract actionable insights with **grep** and **awk**, and address common errors that may arise. By mastering these techniques, you'll be equipped to identify issues early, resolve them quickly, and optimize your USS environment.

Using Logs for Proactive Monitoring

Logs are one of the most valuable resources for monitoring USS workflows. They provide a detailed record of system activity, helping you track performance, detect anomalies, and troubleshoot problems before they escalate.

1. Understanding Log Files:
   USS workflows generate logs in various locations, depending on the task or application. Common log types include:
   - System Logs: Record system-level events, such as process starts and stops.
   - Application Logs: Capture application-specific activity, such as file transfers or script executions.
   - Error Logs: Highlight issues or failures encountered during execution.
2. Best Practices for Log Management:
   - Centralize Logs: Store logs in a dedicated directory for easy access and analysis.
   - Set Up Retention Policies: Regularly archive or delete old logs to prevent clutter.
   - Monitor Logs Regularly: Use scheduled checks to ensure logs remain within expected parameters.
3. Example: Setting Up Log Rotation:
   To prevent log files from growing too large, you can implement log rotation using a simple script:

```
#!/bin/sh

LOG_DIR="/u/user/logs"

find $LOG_DIR -type f -mtime +7 -exec rm {} \;

echo "Old logs deleted."
```

This script deletes log files older than 7 days, keeping storage usage under control.

Tools for Live Log Updates (tail -f)

When troubleshooting or monitoring active processes, real-time visibility into log updates is essential. The **tail -f** command allows you to view log entries as they are written, making it easier to track ongoing activity.

1. How to Use **tail -f**:
   Simply specify the log file you want to monitor:

tail -f /u/user/logs/app.log

The terminal will display new entries as they are appended to the file. Press **Ctrl+C** to stop monitoring.

1. Filtering Specific Entries:
   Combine **tail -f** with **grep** to focus on specific keywords or patterns. For example:

tail -f /u/user/logs/app.log | grep "ERROR"

This command filters only lines containing the word "ERROR," helping you quickly identify issues.

1. Real-World Use Case:
   Imagine you're running a nightly batch job. By monitoring the log file with **tail -f**, you can verify that tasks are completing successfully or identify errors as they occur, enabling faster resolution.

Extracting Insights with grep and awk

Logs often contain vast amounts of data, but not all of it is relevant to your needs. Tools like **grep** and **awk** allow you to filter and analyze log data efficiently, extracting meaningful insights.

1. Using **grep** for Pattern Matching:
   The **grep** command searches for specific patterns within text files. It's particularly useful for isolating relevant log entries.
   - Example:

grep "Completed" /u/user/logs/app.log

This command retrieves all lines containing the word "Completed."

- Advanced Usage:
  You can use regular expressions for more complex searches. For example:

grep -E "ERROR|WARNING" /u/user/logs/app.log

This retrieves lines containing either "ERROR" or "WARNING."

1. Using **awk** for Data Extraction:
   The **awk** command is a powerful tool for processing structured data, such as log files with columns.
   - Example: Extract the timestamp and status from a log file:

awk '{print $1, $5}' /u/user/logs/app.log

This command prints the first (timestamp) and fifth (status) fields from each line.

- Real-World Use Case:
  Suppose your log file contains disk usage metrics. You can calculate average usage with **awk**:

```
awk '{total += $3} END {print "Average:", total/NR}' /u/user/logs/disk_usage.log
```

This calculates the average value of the third column (e.g., disk usage percentage).

1. Combining **grep** and **awk**:
   You can chain commands together for deeper analysis. For example:

```
grep "ERROR" /u/user/logs/app.log | awk '{print $1, $4}'
```

This extracts timestamps and error codes from log entries containing "ERROR."

Common Errors and How to Fix Them

Even with careful planning, errors can occur in USS workflows. Understanding common issues and their solutions will help you troubleshoot effectively.

1. Permission Denied Errors:
   - Cause: Insufficient permissions to access files or directories.
   - Solution: Check and adjust permissions using **chmod** or **chown**.

```
chmod 755 script.sh
chown user1:group1 file.txt
```

1. Command Not Found Errors:
   - Cause: The required utility or script is not installed or not in the PATH.

- Solution: Verify the command exists and add its location to the PATH if necessary.

export PATH=$PATH:/path/to/utility

1. Out of Memory Errors:
    - Cause: A script or process consumes excessive memory.
    - Solution: Optimize resource usage or increase memory allocation. For example, split large tasks into smaller batches:

split -l 1000 largefile.txt part_

1. File Not Found Errors:
    - Cause: A referenced file or directory does not exist.
    - Solution: Double-check file paths and ensure files are present.

ls -l /u/user/input/*.dat

1. Script Syntax Errors:
    - Cause: Mistakes in script syntax, such as missing quotes or semicolons.
    - Solution: Debug the script using **set -x** or validate it with tools like **shellcheck**.

set -x
./script.sh

1. Timeouts or Hangs:
    - Cause: Long-running processes or network delays.
    - Solution: Add timeouts or checkpoints to your

scripts. For example:

timeout 60s ./long_running_process.sh

Why Monitoring and Troubleshooting Matter

Proactive monitoring and effective troubleshooting are essential for maintaining a reliable USS environment. By leveraging logs, tools like **tail -f**, **grep**, and **awk**, and addressing common errors, you can:

- Detect and resolve issues before they impact operations.
- Gain deeper insights into system performance and behavior.
- Build confidence in your ability to manage and optimize USS workflows.

As you apply these techniques, you'll develop a robust skill set for ensuring the success of your modernization initiatives.

With these monitoring and troubleshooting skills in hand, you're now prepared to move on to more advanced topics, such as aligning USS with business goals and executing pilot projects. Keep practicing these tools—they're the foundation of a resilient and efficient USS environment!

Part 2: Aligning USS with Business Goals

Welcome to Part 2: Aligning USS with Business Goals, where we transition from foundational technical skills to the strategic application of z/OS UNIX System Services (USS) within your organization. While mastering commands, scripting, and troubleshooting is essential, the true value of USS lies in its ability to drive measurable business outcomes. This section focuses on how to align USS capabilities with organizational objectives, secure stakeholder buy-in, and position USS as a critical tool for modernization.

Why Focus on Business Alignment?

Technical expertise alone isn't enough to ensure the success of your modernization initiatives. To gain leadership support and drive adoption, you need to demonstrate how USS directly contributes to achieving business goals such as cost reduction, efficiency improvement, and scalability. By connecting USS capabilities to tangible benefits, you can build a compelling case for its adoption and ensure long-term success.

What You'll Learn in This Part

This section is divided into three key chapters, each addressing a critical aspect of aligning USS with business goals:

1. Mapping USS Capabilities to Organizational Objectives
   In this chapter, you'll explore how USS can deliver value across various dimensions of your organization. From

automating repetitive tasks to streamline workflows and scaling solutions for future growth, you'll learn how to identify opportunities where USS can make the greatest impact. You'll also discover how to engage stakeholders who stand to benefit most from USS adoption.

2. Drafting a Modernization Project Proposal
   A well-structured proposal is your blueprint for gaining approval and resources for USS initiatives. This chapter will guide you through crafting a clear and persuasive proposal, complete with problem statements, solution approaches, expected outcomes, and metrics for measuring success. Real-world case studies will illustrate how others have successfully pitched USS projects to leadership.
3. Communicating the Value of USS
   Even the best ideas require effective communication to gain traction. This chapter will teach you how to prepare presentations that highlight the benefits of USS, address objections and misconceptions, and build trust through data and examples. You'll learn how to articulate the value of USS in a way that resonates with both technical and non-technical audiences.

How This Part Fits Into the Bigger Picture

The skills and strategies you'll acquire in this section are essential for bridging the gap between technical implementation and business impact. By aligning USS with organizational objectives, you'll not only justify its adoption but also lay the groundwork for broader modernization efforts. These chapters will empower you to lead initiatives that deliver measurable value, secure ongoing support, and position you as a trusted advocate for innovation within your organization.

By the end of this part, you'll be equipped to translate USS capabilities into actionable strategies that drive business success. With these tools in hand, you'll be ready to move on to executing pilot projects and scaling solutions across your organization.

Let's dive in and explore how USS can transform your business—one objective, proposal, and presentation at a time.

Chapter 6. Mapping USS Capabilities to Organizational Objectives

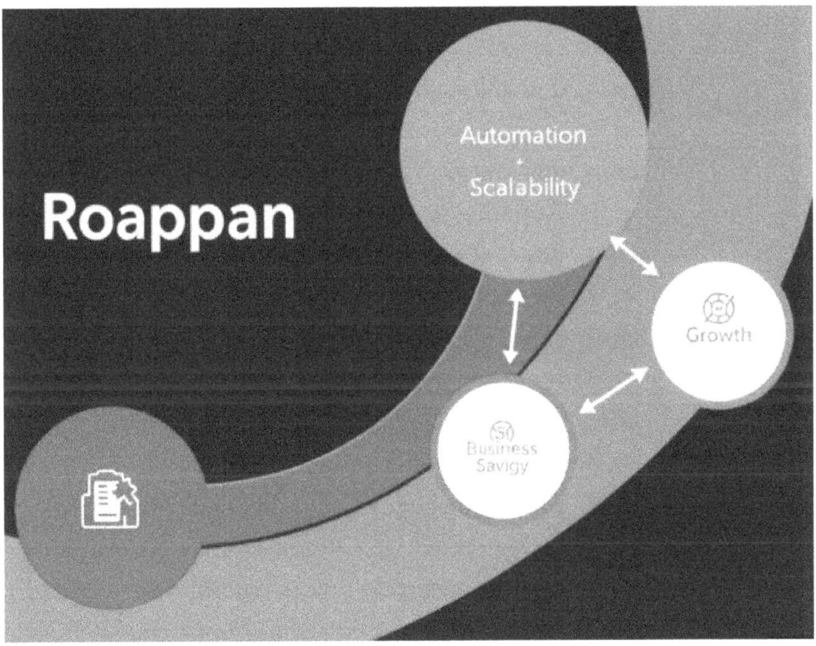

To fully realize the potential of z/OS UNIX System Services (USS), it's essential to align its capabilities with your organization's strategic goals. In this chapter, we'll explore how USS can drive cost reduction through automation, improve efficiency with streamlined workflows, enable scalability for future growth, and identify key stakeholders who stand to benefit from its adoption. By connecting USS to tangible business outcomes, you'll be able to build a compelling case for its implementation and secure leadership support.

Cost Reduction Through Automation

Automation is one of the most powerful ways USS can deliver value to your organization. By automating repetitive, manual tasks, you can significantly reduce labor costs, minimize errors, and free up resources for higher-value activities.

1. Eliminating Manual Effort:
   Many organizations rely on manual processes for tasks like file transfers, data processing, and report generation. These tasks are not only time-consuming but also prone to human error. USS enables you to automate these workflows using shell scripts or scheduling tools, reducing the need for manual intervention.
   - Example: Automating nightly batch jobs can save hours of manual effort each day, allowing IT staff to focus on more strategic initiatives.
2. Reducing Operational Costs:
   Automation directly translates to cost savings. For instance, by automating routine maintenance tasks, you can reduce overtime labor costs and lower the risk of costly errors.
   - Real-World Use Case: A financial institution implemented USS automation for regulatory reporting, cutting processing times by 40% and saving $50,000 annually in labor costs.
3. Measuring Cost Savings:
   To quantify the impact of automation, track metrics such as:
   - Hours saved per task.
   - Reduction in error rates.
   - Decrease in operational expenses.

By focusing on cost reduction, you can demonstrate the financial benefits of USS adoption and secure leadership buy-in.

Efficiency Improvement with Streamlined Workflows

In addition to cost savings, USS can dramatically improve operational efficiency by streamlining workflows and eliminating bottlenecks. This not only enhances productivity but also improves overall system performance.

1. Optimizing Task Execution:
   USS allows you to execute tasks faster and more reliably than traditional methods. For example, integrating USS with JCL workflows ensures seamless execution of batch jobs without manual oversight.
   - Example: A retail company streamlined inventory updates during peak sales periods, reducing processing times by 30% and improving customer satisfaction.
2. Enhancing Cross-Team Collaboration:
   By providing a common platform for file management and scripting, USS fosters collaboration between teams. For instance, IT and operations teams can work together to design and implement efficient workflows that meet both technical and business needs.
3. Leveraging Familiar Tools:
   USS supports scripting languages like Python and shell commands, making it accessible even to teams without extensive Linux expertise. This reduces the learning curve and accelerates adoption.
4. Measuring Efficiency Gains:
   To evaluate workflow improvements, track metrics such as:
   - Processing time reductions.
   - Task completion rates.
   - Resource utilization (e.g., CPU, memory).

Efficiency gains not only enhance day-to-day operations but also position your organization for long-term success.

Scalability for Future Growth

As your organization grows, so do its demands for flexibility, adaptability, and scalability. USS provides the tools you need to scale your workflows and infrastructure without compromising performance or security.

1. Supporting Modular Solutions:
   USS enables modular, scalable solutions that can be easily modified or expanded to meet changing needs. For example, you can start by automating a single process and gradually scale the solution across departments or teams.
   - Example: A healthcare provider used USS to handle increasing data volumes during regulatory reporting cycles, ensuring compliance without requiring additional hardware.
2. Enabling Cross-Platform Integration:
   USS bridges the gap between mainframe and non-mainframe environments, enabling seamless integration with cloud platforms, distributed systems, and third-party applications. This cross-platform capability ensures your workflows remain flexible and future-proof.
   - Real-World Use Case: A manufacturing company integrated USS with cloud-based analytics tools, enabling faster decision-making and supporting global expansion.
3. Planning for Growth:
   To ensure scalability, consider the following:
   - Design workflows with modularity in mind.
   - Test solutions in controlled environments before scaling.

- Monitor resource utilization to identify potential bottlenecks.

Scalability is a key driver of modernization, and USS provides the foundation you need to grow confidently.

Identifying Stakeholders Who Benefit from USS

For any initiative to succeed, it's crucial to identify and engage the stakeholders who will benefit most from USS adoption. These stakeholders can provide valuable input, advocate for the project, and help secure leadership approval.

1. IT Teams:
   IT professionals are often the primary users of USS, leveraging its capabilities to automate tasks, optimize workflows, and troubleshoot issues. By demonstrating how USS simplifies their work, you can gain their support and collaboration.
2. Operations Teams:
   Operations teams rely on efficient workflows to meet deadlines and maintain service levels. USS can streamline their processes, reduce delays, and improve accuracy, making it a valuable tool for their success.
3. Business Leaders:
   Executives and managers care about the bottom line and strategic outcomes. Highlight how USS drives cost savings, improves efficiency, and supports scalability to align with organizational goals.
4. End Users:
   End users, such as employees or customers, benefit indirectly from USS implementations. For example, faster processing times and reduced errors lead to better service delivery and user experiences.

5. Engaging Stakeholders:
   To effectively engage stakeholders:
   - Clearly articulate the benefits of USS for their specific roles.
   - Solicit feedback to ensure their needs are addressed.
   - Share measurable results to build trust and confidence.

By identifying and involving key stakeholders, you can create a coalition of support that drives USS adoption and ensures long-term success.

Why Aligning USS with Business Goals Matters

Mapping USS capabilities to organizational objectives is not just a technical exercise—it's a strategic imperative. By focusing on cost reduction, efficiency improvement, scalability, and stakeholder engagement, you can demonstrate the tangible value of USS and position it as a critical tool for modernization. These efforts will not only justify its adoption but also lay the groundwork for broader transformation initiatives.

With these insights in hand, you're now ready to move on to drafting a modernization project proposal and communicating the value of USS to leadership. Let's continue building the case for USS—one objective at a time.

Chapter 7. Drafting a Modernization Project Proposal

A well-crafted modernization project proposal is your blueprint for gaining leadership approval and resources to implement z/OS UNIX System Services (USS). In this chapter, we'll explore how to structure your proposal effectively, include metrics for measuring success, and draw inspiration from real-world case studies of successful proposals. By the end of this chapter, you'll be equipped to create a persuasive proposal that aligns USS with your organization's strategic goals.

Structuring the Proposal: Problem Statement, Solution Approach, Expected Outcomes

The key to a compelling proposal lies in its structure. A clear and logical flow ensures that stakeholders understand the problem, the proposed solution, and the expected benefits. Here's how to structure your proposal:

1. Problem Statement:
   The problem statement defines the challenge or inefficiency your organization is facing. It should be concise, data-driven, and aligned with business priorities.
   - Key Elements:
     - Clearly articulate the issue.
     - Use data or examples to highlight the impact.
     - Connect the problem to organizational objectives.
   - Example Problem Statement:
     "Currently, nightly batch processing requires significant manual intervention, leading to errors and delays. This has resulted in a 20% increase in overtime labor costs over the past year."
2. Solution Approach:
   The solution approach outlines how USS will address the identified problem. Focus on practical, actionable steps that demonstrate feasibility and value.
   - Key Elements:
     - Describe the tools and technologies (e.g., USS scripts, Python).
     - Highlight integration with existing systems.
     - Emphasize scalability and flexibility.

    - Example Solution Approach:
      "To address the issue, we propose automating nightly batch jobs using USS scripts. These scripts will process datasets, generate reports, and archive results without manual intervention."
3. Expected Outcomes:
   Expected outcomes define the measurable benefits stakeholders can expect. Be specific and tie outcomes to business goals such as cost reduction, efficiency improvement, and scalability.
    - Key Elements:
        - Include quantifiable metrics (e.g., reduced processing time, lower operational costs).
        - Highlight both short-term and long-term benefits.
        - Align outcomes with stakeholder priorities.
    - Example Expected Outcomes:
        - Reduce nightly batch processing time by 30%.
        - Lower operational costs by eliminating overtime labor.
        - Improve data accuracy and reliability, reducing errors by 25%.

By structuring your proposal with these elements, you'll create a clear and compelling case for USS adoption.

Including Metrics for Measuring Success

Metrics are the backbone of any successful proposal. They provide a way to quantify the impact of your initiative and demonstrate its value to stakeholders. When including metrics, focus on those that directly align with organizational goals.

1. Common Metrics for USS Projects:
    - Processing Time Reductions: Measure the time saved by automating tasks.
        - Example Metric: "Nightly batch jobs now complete in 2 hours instead of 3, reducing processing time by 33%."
    - Error Rate Improvements: Track reductions in errors due to automation.
        - Example Metric: "Nightly batch job errors decreased from 10 per week to 2, improving accuracy by 80%."
    - Resource Utilization: Monitor CPU, memory, and other system resources used during task execution.
        - Example Metric: "CPU usage for nightly batch jobs decreased from 80% to 50%, freeing resources for other tasks."
2. Linking Metrics to Business Goals:
   Ensure your metrics resonate with stakeholders by connecting them to tangible business outcomes. For example:
    - Cost savings: "Reduced processing times save $50,000 annually in labor costs."
    - Efficiency gains: "Streamlined workflows improve throughput by 40%."
    - Scalability: "Modular design allows for expansion to additional teams with minimal effort."
3. Visualizing Metrics:
   Use charts, graphs, and tables to present your metrics in an easily digestible format. Visuals make your case more relatable and memorable.
    - Example: A bar chart showing a 33% reduction in nightly batch processing times after USS implementation.

By including metrics, you'll provide stakeholders with concrete evidence of USS's value and build confidence in your proposal.

Real-World Case Studies of Successful Proposals

Learning from real-world examples can inspire your own proposal and demonstrate what works in practice. Below are two case studies of organizations that successfully pitched USS projects to leadership.

1. Case Study 1: Financial Institution Automates Regulatory Reporting
    - Problem Statement:
      The institution faced increasing regulatory reporting requirements, leading to delays and errors in manual processes.
    - Solution Approach:
      Implemented USS automation to streamline data processing and report generation. Scripts were integrated with existing JCL workflows to ensure compatibility.
    - Expected Outcomes:
        - Reduced processing times by 40%.
        - Eliminated manual errors, improving compliance.
        - Saved $50,000 annually in overtime labor costs.
    - Outcome:
      Leadership approved the project, citing measurable improvements in efficiency and cost savings. The success of the pilot led to broader adoption across departments.
2. Case Study 2: Retail Company Streamlines Inventory Updates
    - Problem Statement:

Manual inventory updates during peak sales periods caused delays and customer dissatisfaction.

- Solution Approach:
  Automated inventory updates using USS scripts, ensuring real-time data availability. Integrated with cloud-based analytics tools for faster decision-making.
- Expected Outcomes:
  - Reduced processing times by 30%.
  - Improved customer satisfaction scores by 15%.
  - Increased sales during peak periods due to faster updates.
- Outcome:
  The proposal secured funding and executive support. The pilot project's success led to enterprise-wide implementation.

These case studies illustrate how a well-structured proposal, supported by metrics and real-world examples, can drive USS adoption and deliver measurable value.

Why a Strong Proposal Matters

A strong modernization project proposal serves as your foundation for securing leadership approval and resources. By clearly articulating the problem, solution, and expected outcomes—and supporting them with metrics—you can build a compelling case for USS adoption. Real-world examples further reinforce the feasibility and value of your initiative, inspiring confidence among stakeholders.

With these tools and insights, you're now ready to draft a proposal that aligns USS with your organization's goals and secures the support needed for success. Let's continue building the case for USS—one proposal at a time.

Chapter 8. Communicating the Value of USS

Effectively communicating the value of z/OS UNIX System Services (USS) is essential for gaining stakeholder buy-in and driving adoption. In this chapter, we'll explore how to prepare presentations that highlight USS benefits, address objections and misconceptions, and build trust through data and real-world examples. By mastering these skills, you'll be able to articulate the value of USS in a way that resonates with both technical and non-technical audiences.

Preparing Presentations That Highlight USS Benefits

A well-prepared presentation can make or break your ability to communicate the value of USS. The key is to focus on the benefits that matter most to your audience and present them in a clear, engaging manner.

1. Start with the Big Picture:
   Begin by framing USS as a solution to specific business challenges. Connect its capabilities to organizational goals such as cost reduction, efficiency improvement, and scalability.
   - Example Opening Statement:
     "USS enables us to automate repetitive tasks, streamline workflows, and integrate seamlessly with cloud platforms—delivering measurable value to our organization."
2. Highlight Key Benefits:
   Focus on the benefits that align with stakeholder priorities. Common USS benefits include:
   - Flexibility: Modular solutions that adapt to changing needs.
   - Cross-Platform Integration: Bridging the gap between mainframe and non-mainframe environments.
   - Cost Savings: Automating manual tasks to reduce labor costs and errors.
   - Efficiency Gains: Streamlining workflows to improve throughput and performance.
   - Example Talking Points:
     - "With USS, we can leverage familiar scripting languages like Python to process datasets, bridging the gap between our mainframe and cloud environments."
     - "Our pilot project reduced nightly batch

processing time by 30%, saving $50,000 annually in overtime labor costs."

3. Use Visuals to Tell the Story:
   Visual aids make your presentation more engaging and memorable. Use charts, graphs, and diagrams to illustrate key points.
   - Example Visual:
     A bar chart showing a 40% reduction in error rates after implementing USS automation.
   - Best Practices:
     - Keep visuals simple and focused on key metrics.
     - Use color coding and labels to enhance clarity.
     - Include before-and-after comparisons to highlight improvements.
4. Tailor Your Message to the Audience:
   Adjust your presentation based on the audience's level of technical expertise. For example:
   - With IT teams: Dive into technical details like scripting tools and integration capabilities.
   - With business leaders: Focus on high-level outcomes like cost savings and efficiency gains.

By preparing a presentation that highlights USS benefits in a way that resonates with your audience, you'll build enthusiasm and support for your initiative.

Addressing Objections and Misconceptions

Even the most compelling presentation may face objections or misconceptions about USS adoption. Addressing these proactively demonstrates your preparedness and builds confidence among stakeholders.

1. Common Objections and How to Address Them:
    - Objection: USS Requires Full Linux Expertise
        - Response:
          "USS is designed for z/OS users and does not require full Linux expertise. It supports familiar scripting languages like Python and shell commands, making it accessible even without extensive Linux skills."
        - Real-World Example:
          A healthcare provider successfully implemented USS automation using scripts written by their existing IT team, who had no prior Linux experience.
    - Concern: Implementation Will Disrupt Operations
        - Response:
          "USS integrates seamlessly with existing JCL workflows, allowing us to implement changes incrementally without disrupting operations."
        - Real-World Example:
          A financial institution tested USS automation during off-peak hours, ensuring minimal impact while achieving measurable improvements.
    - Doubt: USS Won't Deliver Measurable Value
        - Response:
          "Our pilot project demonstrated a 30% reduction in nightly batch processing times and a 25% decrease in operational costs, aligning with our goal of improving efficiency."
        - Real-World Example:
          A retail company used USS to streamline inventory updates during peak sales periods, improving customer satisfaction and increasing revenue.

2. Proactive Communication:
   Anticipate potential concerns and address them early in your presentation. This shows stakeholders that you've thoughtfully considered their perspectives and are prepared to mitigate risks.
3. Building Confidence Through Transparency:
   Be honest about potential challenges and outline your plan to address them. For example:
   - "While there may be a learning curve for some team members, we've developed training materials and will provide hands-on support to ensure a smooth transition."

By addressing objections and misconceptions upfront, you'll build trust and demonstrate your commitment to success.

Building Trust Through Data and Examples

Data and real-world examples are powerful tools for building trust and credibility. They provide tangible evidence of USS's value and help stakeholders visualize its impact.

1. Using Metrics to Build Credibility:
   Quantifiable metrics are the most persuasive way to demonstrate USS's value. Use data from pilot projects, case studies, or industry benchmarks to support your claims.
   - Example Metrics:
     - Processing time reductions: "Nightly batch jobs now complete in 2 hours instead of 3, reducing processing time by 33%."
     - Error rate improvements: "Nightly batch job errors decreased from 10 per week to 2, improving accuracy by 80%."
     - Cost savings: "Automating regulatory

reporting saved $50,000 annually in labor costs."

2. Sharing Real-World Examples:
   Real-world examples make your case relatable and credible. Share stories of organizations that have successfully implemented USS, highlighting measurable outcomes and lessons learned.
   - Example Case Study:
     "A manufacturing company integrated USS with cloud-based analytics tools, enabling faster decision-making and supporting global expansion. This resulted in a 20% increase in operational efficiency."
3. Leveraging Testimonials:
   If possible, include testimonials from colleagues, partners, or industry experts who have experienced the benefits of USS firsthand.
   - Example Testimonial:
     "Implementing USS automation has been a game-changer for our team. We've reduced processing times, eliminated errors, and freed up resources for higher-value activities."
4. Connecting Data to Business Goals:
   Ensure your data and examples align with stakeholder priorities. For instance:
   - Cost-conscious executives: Highlight cost savings and ROI.
   - Operations teams: Emphasize efficiency gains and error reductions.
   - End users: Focus on improved service delivery and user experiences.

By building trust through data and examples, you'll create a compelling case for USS adoption that resonates with stakeholders at all levels.

Why Effective Communication Matters

Communicating the value of USS is not just about presenting facts—it's about inspiring action. By preparing presentations that highlight USS benefits, addressing objections and misconceptions, and building trust through data and examples, you'll position yourself as a trusted advocate for modernization. These efforts will not only secure leadership approval but also drive broader adoption across your organization.

With these communication strategies in hand, you're now ready to execute pilot projects and scale USS solutions with confidence. Let's continue building momentum for USS—one conversation at a time.

Part 3: Executing and Scaling USS Initiatives

Welcome to Part 3: Executing and Scaling USS Initiatives , where we transition from planning and communication to the practical execution of your modernization efforts. This section focuses on turning ideas into action—starting with a pilot project, measuring its success, and scaling the solution across your organization. By the end of this part, you'll have the tools and strategies needed to take USS from a small-scale proof of concept to an enterprise-wide transformation.

Why Focus on Execution and Scaling?

While aligning USS with business goals and securing stakeholder buy-in are critical first steps, the true test of any modernization initiative lies in its execution. A well-executed pilot project demonstrates feasibility, builds confidence, and provides valuable insights for broader adoption. Similarly, scaling USS requires strategic planning, effective change management, and a focus on long-term sustainability. These chapters will equip you with the skills to execute initiatives successfully and ensure lasting impact.

What You'll Learn in This Part

This section is divided into three key chapters, each addressing a critical phase of executing and scaling USS initiatives:

1. Planning and Implementing a Pilot Project
   In this chapter, you'll learn how to design and execute a small-scale pilot project to demonstrate USS feasibility. From

defining the scope and identifying stakeholders to setting objectives and monitoring performance, you'll gain the tools to test USS in a controlled environment and gather actionable feedback.

2. Measuring and Reporting Results
   Once your pilot project is complete, it's time to measure its impact and communicate the results to leadership. This chapter will guide you through tracking KPIs like task completion rates and resource utilization, presenting findings effectively, and securing ongoing support for broader adoption.
3. Scaling Up: From Pilot to Enterprise-Wide Implementation
   Scaling USS requires more than just replicating the pilot—it involves adapting the solution to meet the needs of different teams, managing resistance to change, and ensuring long-term success. This chapter will explore strategies for expanding USS adoption while maintaining efficiency, reliability, and alignment with organizational goals.

How This Part Fits Into the Bigger Picture

The skills and strategies you'll acquire in this section are essential for bridging the gap between theory and practice. By executing a pilot project, you'll validate the value of USS in a real-world context. By measuring and reporting results, you'll build a compelling case for scaling the solution. And by focusing on scalability and change management, you'll ensure that USS becomes a cornerstone of your organization's modernization strategy. Together, these chapters provide a roadmap for driving sustainable, enterprise-wide transformation.

By the end of this part, you'll be equipped to execute USS initiatives confidently and scale them effectively, positioning your organization for long-term success. With these tools in hand, you'll be ready to tackle advanced topics and continue your journey toward mastering mainframe modernization.

Let's dive in and explore how to turn your USS vision into reality—one step at a time.

Chapter 9. Planning and Implementing a Pilot Project

A pilot project is a critical step in demonstrating the feasibility of z/OS UNIX System Services (USS) while minimizing risk and resource investment. In this chapter, we'll explore how to define the scope of your pilot, identify resources and stakeholders, set clear objectives and metrics, and monitor performance while collecting feedback. By following these steps, you'll create a controlled environment to test USS capabilities and gather insights that will guide broader adoption.

Defining the Scope of the Pilot

The first step in planning a successful pilot project is defining its scope. A well-defined scope ensures that the project remains manageable, focused, and aligned with organizational goals.

1. Choose a Specific Process or Task:
   Start by identifying a specific process or task that can benefit from USS automation. This could be anything from nightly batch processing to file transfers or dataset updates.
   - Example: Automating regulatory reporting workflows for the finance department.
2. Limit the Scope to a Single Department or Team:
   To minimize complexity and ensure focus, limit the pilot to a single department or team. This allows you to test USS in a controlled environment while building confidence among stakeholders.
   - Example: Piloting USS automation for the inventory management team during peak sales periods.
3. Set Boundaries for the Pilot:
   Clearly define what is included—and excluded—from the pilot. For example, if automating nightly batch jobs, specify which datasets and workflows will be covered.
   - Example Scope Statement:
     "The pilot will focus on automating nightly inventory updates using USS scripts, limited to the retail operations team."
4. Align the Scope with Business Goals:
   Ensure the pilot addresses a specific business challenge or inefficiency. This alignment will make it easier to justify the initiative and demonstrate its value.
   - Example Alignment:
     "By automating inventory updates, we aim to reduce processing

times by 30% and improve data accuracy during peak sales periods."

By defining the scope clearly, you'll create a focused and achievable pilot project that lays the foundation for success.

Identifying Resources and Stakeholders

A successful pilot project requires the right resources and stakeholder engagement. Identifying these early ensures smooth execution and builds support for broader adoption.

1. Assign Roles and Responsibilities:
   Clearly define who will be responsible for each aspect of the pilot. This includes:
    - Project Lead: Oversees the pilot and ensures alignment with objectives.
    - Technical Team: Implements and tests USS automation.
    - End Users: Provide feedback on usability and impact.
    - Example Role Assignment:
      "The IT team will develop and test USS scripts, while the operations team will validate results and provide feedback."
2. Engage Key Stakeholders:
   Identify stakeholders who will benefit from the pilot and involve them early in the process. These may include:
    - Business Leaders: Approve the initiative and allocate resources.
    - Department Managers: Provide input on requirements and priorities.
    - End Users: Test the solution and share feedback.
    - Example Stakeholder Engagement:

"The finance team will provide input on regulatory reporting requirements, while the IT team implements the USS automation."

3. Secure Necessary Resources:
   Ensure you have access to the tools, systems, and personnel needed for the pilot. This may include:
   - Access to USS environments and utilities.
   - Time and budget for development and testing.
   - Training materials for end users.

By identifying resources and stakeholders upfront, you'll ensure the pilot has the support and resources it needs to succeed.

Setting Clear Objectives and Metrics

Clear objectives and measurable metrics are essential for evaluating the success of your pilot project. They provide a framework for assessing performance and demonstrating value.

1. Define Measurable Objectives:
   Set specific, achievable goals that align with business priorities. For example:
   - Reduce nightly batch processing time by 25%.
   - Eliminate manual errors in file transfers.
   - Improve resource utilization by 20%.
   - Example Objective:
     "Automate nightly inventory updates to reduce processing time by 30% and eliminate manual intervention errors."
2. Track Key Performance Indicators (KPIs):
   Use KPIs to measure the impact of the pilot. Common metrics include:
   - Processing Time Reductions: Measure time saved by automating tasks.

  - Error Rate Improvements: Track reductions in errors due to automation.
  - Resource Utilization: Monitor CPU, memory, and other system resources used during task execution.
  - Example Metrics:
    - Processing time reduced from 3 hours to 2 hours.
    - Error rates decreased from 10 per week to 2.
    - CPU usage dropped from 80% to 50%.
3. Connect Metrics to Business Outcomes:
   Ensure your metrics resonate with stakeholders by linking them to tangible business outcomes. For example:
   - Cost savings: "Reduced processing times save $50,000 annually in labor costs."
   - Efficiency gains: "Streamlined workflows improve throughput by 40%."
   - Scalability: "Modular design allows for expansion to additional teams with minimal effort."

By setting clear objectives and metrics, you'll create a roadmap for success and provide stakeholders with concrete evidence of USS's value.

Monitoring Performance and Collecting Feedback

Once the pilot is underway, monitoring performance and collecting feedback are critical for ensuring success and gathering insights for broader adoption.

1. Monitor Performance in Real-Time:
   Use logs and diagnostic tools to track performance during the pilot. Tools like **tail -f**, **grep**, and **awk** can help you identify trends, detect issues, and measure progress against objectives.
   - Example Monitoring:

"Use **tail -f** to monitor log files and ensure nightly batch jobs complete without errors."

2. Address Issues Promptly:
   If problems arise, address them quickly to maintain stakeholder confidence. For example:
   - Adjust script timeout settings to handle larger datasets.
   - Optimize resource usage to prevent bottlenecks.
   - Example Adjustment:
     "Increased memory allocation to address performance issues during peak processing times."
3. Collect Feedback from Stakeholders:
   Gather feedback from end users and stakeholders to identify areas for improvement. Use surveys, interviews, or informal discussions to capture qualitative insights.
   - Example Feedback Collection:
     "The operations team reports that automated inventory updates are faster but suggest adding error notifications for failed tasks."
4. Document Lessons Learned:
   Document successes, challenges, and lessons learned during the pilot. This documentation will guide future projects and ensure scalability.
   - Example Documentation:
     "Pilot demonstrated a 30% reduction in processing times but highlighted the need for error notifications."

By monitoring performance and collecting feedback, you'll ensure the pilot meets its objectives while gathering valuable insights for scaling the solution.

Why a Well-Executed Pilot Matters

A well-executed pilot project is the foundation of broader USS adoption. By defining the scope, identifying resources and stakeholders, setting clear objectives and metrics, and monitoring performance, you'll demonstrate the feasibility and value of USS in a real-world context. These efforts will build confidence among stakeholders and provide a roadmap for scaling the solution across your organization.

With these tools and strategies in hand, you're now ready to measure and report the results of your pilot project. Let's continue driving momentum for USS—one pilot at a time.

Chapter 10. Measuring and Reporting Results

Measuring and reporting the results of your USS pilot project is a critical step in securing ongoing support for broader adoption. In this chapter, we'll explore how to track key performance indicators (KPIs) like task completion rates and resource utilization, present findings effectively to leadership, and build a case for scaling USS across your organization. By mastering these skills, you'll ensure that the value of USS is clearly communicated and recognized.

Tracking KPIs Like Task Completion Rates and Resource Utilization

Tracking KPIs provides measurable evidence of the pilot project's success and helps quantify its impact on efficiency, cost savings, and system performance. Here's how to identify and measure the most relevant KPIs:

1. Task Completion Rates:
   Task completion rates measure how efficiently tasks are completed after USS implementation. Compare pre- and post-pilot metrics to demonstrate improvements.
   - Example Metric:
     "Nightly batch jobs now complete in 2 hours instead of 3, reducing processing time by 33%."
   - Tools for Tracking:
     Use logs and monitoring tools to measure task durations and completion times.
2. Error Rates:
   Error rates highlight the reliability of USS automation by tracking the frequency of errors during task execution. A reduction in errors demonstrates improved accuracy.
   - Example Metric:
     "Nightly batch job errors decreased from 10 per week to 2, improving accuracy by 80%."
   - Tools for Tracking:
     Analyze log files using commands like **grep** to count and categorize errors.
3. Resource Utilization:
   Resource utilization measures CPU, memory, and other system resources used during task execution. Improved resource usage indicates greater efficiency.
   - Example Metric:

"CPU usage for nightly batch jobs decreased from 80% to 50%, freeing resources for other tasks."
   - Tools for Tracking:
     Use system monitoring utilities or scripts to capture resource usage data before and after implementation.
4. Cost Savings:
   Quantify cost reductions resulting from automation, such as labor savings or reduced overtime expenses.
   - Example Metric:
     "Automating regulatory reporting saved $50,000 annually in labor costs."
   - Tools for Tracking:
     Calculate labor hours saved and multiply by average hourly rates to estimate cost savings.

By tracking these KPIs, you'll create a data-driven narrative that highlights the tangible benefits of USS adoption.

Presenting Findings to Leadership

Effectively presenting your findings is essential for gaining leadership approval and securing resources for broader adoption. Follow these best practices to craft a persuasive presentation:

1. Structure Your Presentation Logically:
   Organize your presentation into clear sections to guide stakeholders through the findings:
   - Executive Summary: Briefly summarize the objectives, approach, and outcomes.
   - KPI Highlights: Present measurable improvements using visuals like charts and graphs.
   - Impact on Business Goals: Connect results to organizational priorities like cost reduction, efficiency improvement, and scalability.

- Next Steps: Outline plans for expanding USS adoption.
- Example Executive Summary:
  "Our pilot project demonstrated a 30% reduction in processing times and a 25% decrease in operational costs, aligning with our goal of improving efficiency."

2. Use Visuals to Enhance Understanding:
   Visual aids make your findings more relatable and memorable. Use bar charts, line graphs, and pie charts to illustrate key points.
   - Example Visual:
     A bar chart showing a 33% reduction in nightly batch processing times after USS implementation.
   - Best Practices:
     - Keep visuals simple and focused on key metrics.
     - Use color coding and labels to enhance clarity.
     - Include before-and-after comparisons to highlight improvements.
3. Connect Data to Stakeholder Priorities:
   Tailor your presentation to resonate with leadership's concerns and priorities. For example:
   - Cost-conscious executives: Highlight cost savings and ROI.
   - Operations teams: Emphasize efficiency gains and error reductions.
   - End users: Focus on improved service delivery and user experiences.
   - Example Talking Point:
     "By automating nightly inventory updates, we've

reduced processing times by 30% and eliminated manual errors, directly supporting our goal of improving customer satisfaction."

4. Anticipate Questions and Address Concerns:
   Be prepared to answer questions about scalability, potential risks, and next steps. Proactively addressing concerns builds confidence in your proposal.
   - Example Response:
     "We've identified scalability opportunities and developed a roadmap for expanding USS automation to additional teams."

By presenting findings clearly and persuasively, you'll demonstrate the value of USS and secure leadership buy-in for broader adoption.

Securing Ongoing Support for Broader Adoption

To ensure the long-term success of USS initiatives, it's essential to secure ongoing support from leadership and stakeholders. Here's how to build momentum and advocate for broader adoption:

1. Highlight Success Stories:
   Share real-world examples of how the pilot project delivered measurable value. Success stories make the case for scaling USS more compelling.
   - Example Success Story:
     "A retail company streamlined inventory updates during peak sales periods, reducing processing times by 30% and improving customer satisfaction scores by 15%."
2. Demonstrate Scalability:
   Show how the solution can be adapted and expanded to meet the needs of different teams or departments. Highlight modular design and integration capabilities.
   - Example Scalability Argument:
     "The pilot project's modular design allows us to scale USS

automation to additional workflows with minimal effort."

3. Outline a Roadmap for Expansion:
   Provide a clear plan for scaling USS adoption, including timelines, resource requirements, and expected outcomes. This demonstrates your commitment to long-term success.
   - Example Roadmap:
     "Phase 1: Expand USS automation to the finance department within three months. Phase 2: Roll out solutions to additional teams over six months."
4. Build Trust Through Transparency:
   Be honest about potential challenges and outline your plan to address them. This shows stakeholders that you've thoughtfully considered their perspectives and are prepared to mitigate risks.
   - Example Transparency Statement:
     "While there may be a learning curve for some team members, we've developed training materials and will provide hands-on support to ensure a smooth transition."
5. Leverage Stakeholder Advocacy:
   Engage early adopters and champions to advocate for USS adoption. Their firsthand experience and enthusiasm can inspire others to embrace the solution.
   - Example Advocacy:
     "The operations team reports that automated inventory updates have significantly improved their workflow, and they're eager to see the solution expanded."

By securing ongoing support, you'll ensure that USS becomes a cornerstone of your organization's modernization strategy, driving sustainable transformation and delivering lasting value.

Why Measuring and Reporting Matter

Measuring and reporting the results of your USS pilot project is not just about demonstrating success—it's about building trust, securing resources, and laying the groundwork for broader adoption. By tracking KPIs, presenting findings effectively, and advocating for ongoing support, you'll position yourself as a leader in modernization efforts and ensure the long-term success of USS initiatives.

With these strategies in hand, you're now ready to scale USS adoption across your organization. Let's continue driving momentum for USS—one milestone at a time.

Chapter 11. Scaling Up: From Pilot to Enterprise-Wide Implementation

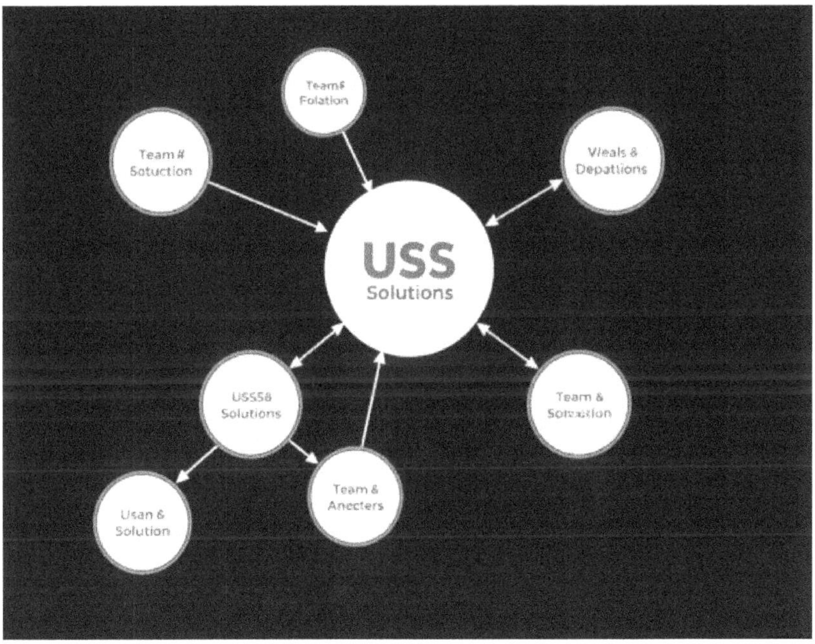

Scaling USS from a pilot project to an enterprise-wide implementation is the ultimate goal of modernization initiatives. However, scaling requires more than simply replicating the pilot—it involves adapting the solution to meet the needs of different teams, managing resistance to change, and ensuring long-term sustainability. In this chapter, we'll explore strategies for expanding USS adoption, overcoming resistance, and ensuring that your efforts deliver lasting value.

Strategies for Expanding USS Across Teams

Expanding USS across teams requires careful planning and execution. Here are key strategies to ensure a smooth and successful rollout:

1. Adapt the Solution to Meet Team-Specific Needs:
   While the pilot project may have addressed a specific process or department, other teams may have unique requirements. Customize the solution to align with their workflows and priorities.
   - Example Adaptation:
     "For the finance team, we added error notifications to improve transparency during regulatory reporting."
2. Leverage Modular Design for Scalability:
   A modular design allows you to scale USS automation incrementally, reducing complexity and minimizing disruption. Use reusable scripts and templates to streamline implementation across teams.
   - Example Modular Approach:
     "We created reusable scripts for file transfers, enabling quick deployment in multiple departments."
3. Roll Out in Phases:
   Avoid overwhelming the organization by rolling out USS in phases. Start with teams or processes that will benefit most, then gradually expand to others.
   - Example Phased Rollout:
     "Phase 1: Implement USS automation for nightly batch jobs in the operations team. Phase 2: Expand to the finance and marketing teams."
4. Provide Training and Support:
   Equip teams with the knowledge and tools they need to adopt USS successfully. Offer hands-on training sessions, user

guides, and ongoing support to address questions and concerns.

  - Example Training Plan:
    "Conduct a two-hour workshop on writing and executing USS scripts, followed by one-on-one mentoring for each team."

5. Communicate Benefits Clearly:
   Highlight how USS will improve efficiency, reduce errors, and save time for each team. Tailor your messaging to resonate with their specific challenges and goals.
   - Example Communication:
     "USS automation will reduce manual intervention in your daily tasks, freeing up time for higher-value activities."

By adopting these strategies, you'll ensure that USS adoption is scalable, adaptable, and aligned with the needs of different teams.

Managing Change and Overcoming Resistance

Resistance to change is a common challenge when scaling new technologies like USS. Proactively addressing concerns and fostering a culture of innovation can help overcome resistance and build enthusiasm for USS adoption.

1. Anticipate Common Concerns:
   Understand the reasons behind resistance and address them proactively. Common concerns include:
   - Fear of job displacement: Reassure employees that USS will enhance their roles, not replace them.
   - Learning curve: Provide training and resources to ease the transition.
   - Disruption to workflows: Emphasize incremental implementation to minimize disruption.
   - Example Response to Concern:
     "USS automation will handle repetitive tasks,

allowing you to focus on more strategic and creative work."

2. Involve Stakeholders Early:
   Engage stakeholders from the outset to ensure their input is considered and their concerns are addressed. This fosters ownership and buy-in.
   - Example Engagement:
     "We held a brainstorming session with the finance team to identify opportunities for USS automation in their workflows."
3. Highlight Success Stories:
   Share real-world examples of how USS has delivered value in the pilot project or other departments. Success stories inspire confidence and demonstrate feasibility.
   - Example Success Story:
     "The operations team reduced nightly batch processing times by 30%, improving throughput and accuracy."
4. Foster a Culture of Innovation:
   Encourage teams to embrace change by highlighting the benefits of modernization and celebrating milestones along the way.
   - Example Celebration:
     "We recognized the IT team's efforts by hosting a 'Modernization Milestone' event to celebrate the successful rollout of USS automation."
5. Provide Ongoing Support:
   Ensure teams feel supported throughout the transition by offering resources like FAQs, troubleshooting guides, and dedicated help desks.
   - Example Support:
     "We set up a USS support hotline and created a shared repository of best practices for teams to reference."

By managing change effectively, you'll create an environment where USS adoption thrives, and teams feel empowered to embrace innovation.

Ensuring Long-Term Success

To ensure the long-term success of USS initiatives, it's essential to focus on sustainability, continuous improvement, and alignment with organizational goals. Here's how to achieve lasting impact:

1. Monitor Performance Continuously:
   Regularly track KPIs like task completion rates, error rates, and resource utilization to ensure USS continues to deliver value. Use monitoring tools and logs to detect issues early.
   - Example Monitoring:
     "Use **tail -f** to monitor log files and ensure nightly batch jobs complete without errors."
2. Refine and Optimize Solutions:
   Gather feedback from users and stakeholders to identify areas for improvement. Refine scripts, workflows, and processes to optimize performance and usability.
   - Example Refinement:
     "Based on user feedback, we added email notifications for failed tasks to improve transparency."
3. Align with Evolving Business Goals:
   As organizational priorities shift, adapt USS solutions to remain relevant and impactful. Regularly review objectives and metrics to ensure alignment.
   - Example Alignment:
     "We updated our USS automation to support new compliance requirements introduced by recent regulations."
4. Build a Community of Practice:
   Foster collaboration and knowledge-sharing among teams by creating a community of practice. Host regular meetings,

workshops, or forums to exchange ideas and best practices.

  - Example Community:
    "We launched a monthly 'USS Innovation Forum' where teams share success stories and lessons learned."

5. Plan for Future Growth:
   Anticipate future needs and plan for scalability. Ensure your USS solutions are flexible enough to accommodate new workflows, teams, or technologies.
   - Example Growth Planning:
     "We designed our USS scripts to integrate seamlessly with cloud platforms, enabling future hybrid workflows."

By focusing on sustainability and continuous improvement, you'll ensure that USS remains a cornerstone of your organization's modernization strategy for years to come.

Why Scaling Matters

Scaling USS from a pilot project to enterprise-wide implementation is the culmination of your modernization efforts. By adopting scalable strategies, managing resistance effectively, and ensuring long-term success, you'll position USS as a transformative tool that drives efficiency, cost savings, and innovation across your organization.

With these strategies in hand, you're now equipped to lead the charge in scaling USS adoption and achieving sustainable transformation. Let's continue driving momentum for USS—one step at a time.

Part 4: Advanced Topics and Best Practices

Welcome to Part 4: Advanced Topics and Best Practices, where we delve into the next level of expertise in z/OS UNIX System Services (USS). This section is designed for learners who have mastered the foundational skills and are ready to explore advanced techniques, optimization strategies, and security considerations that will elevate their USS implementations to new heights.

Modernization is not just about adopting USS—it's about using it effectively, securely, and efficiently to drive innovation and value across your organization. In this part, we'll cover advanced integration techniques, performance optimization strategies, and best practices for securing sensitive data. These topics will empower you to push the boundaries of what USS can achieve while ensuring compliance, scalability, and long-term success.

Why Focus on Advanced Topics and Best Practices?

As you scale USS adoption and tackle more complex challenges, you'll encounter scenarios that require deeper knowledge and specialized skills. Whether you're integrating USS with other technologies, optimizing scripts for peak performance, or safeguarding sensitive data, these advanced topics will equip you to address real-world complexities confidently. Additionally, adhering to best practices ensures that your USS implementations remain secure, efficient, and aligned with industry standards.

What You'll Learn in This Part

This section is divided into three key chapters, each addressing a critical area of advanced USS usage:

1. Integrating USS with Other Technologies
   Explore how USS bridges the gap between traditional mainframe workflows and modern computing environments. Learn to integrate USS with JCL workflows, leverage Python and shell scripts for enhanced automation, and enable cross-platform integration with cloud environments.
2. Optimizing USS for Performance
   Dive into strategies for improving the efficiency of your USS workflows. From reducing resource utilization to writing optimized scripts, this chapter will help you avoid common pitfalls and ensure your solutions perform at their best.
3. Security Considerations in USS
   Security is paramount in any IT environment. This chapter covers best practices for managing file and directory permissions, protecting sensitive data, and ensuring compliance through auditing and monitoring.

How This Part Fits Into the Bigger Picture

The skills and knowledge you'll gain in this section are essential for taking your USS expertise to the next level. By mastering advanced integration, optimization, and security practices, you'll be better equipped to lead large-scale modernization initiatives, troubleshoot complex issues, and position yourself as a trusted expert within your organization. These chapters provide the tools you need to maximize the value of USS while maintaining reliability and compliance.

By the end of this part, you'll have a comprehensive understanding of how to leverage USS in sophisticated, real-world scenarios. With these advanced skills in hand, you'll be ready to tackle the most challenging aspects of mainframe modernization and continue your journey toward mastery.

Let's dive in and explore how to unlock the full potential of USS—one advanced topic at a time.

Chapter 12. Integrating USS with Other Technologies

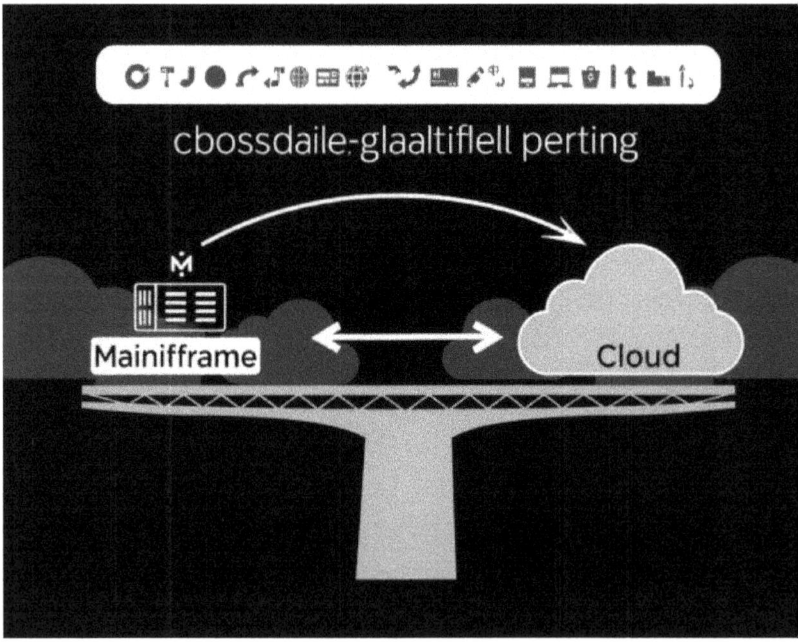

To fully harness the power of z/OS UNIX System Services (USS), it's essential to integrate it with other technologies and workflows. In this chapter, we'll explore how to bridge USS with traditional JCL workflows, leverage Python and shell scripts for enhanced automation, and enable cross-platform integration with cloud environments. By mastering these techniques, you'll create seamless, flexible solutions that maximize the value of USS in your organization.

Bridging USS and JCL Workflows

JCL (Job Control Language) has long been the backbone of mainframe operations, but its capabilities can be extended by integrating with USS. Bridging USS and JCL workflows allows you to combine the familiarity of JCL with the flexibility of USS scripting, creating hybrid solutions that improve efficiency and scalability.

1. Understanding the Integration:
   USS can be invoked from JCL jobs using utilities like **BPXBATCH** or **BPXWDYN**, enabling you to execute shell scripts or commands within a JCL workflow. This integration is particularly useful for automating tasks that require both USS and JCL capabilities.
   - Example Use Case:
     "A nightly batch job uses JCL to process datasets and invokes a USS script to generate reports and archive results."
2. Using BPXBATCH for Script Execution:
   The **BPXBATCH** utility allows you to run USS commands or scripts as part of a JCL job. Here's an example:

//**STEP01 EXEC PGM=BPXBATCH**

//**STDPARM DD** *

SH /u/user/scripts/process_data.sh

/*

This JCL step executes a USS shell script (**process_data.sh**) to handle specific tasks.

1. Passing Data Between JCL and USS:
   You can pass data between JCL and USS workflows using files or environment variables. For example, JCL can write

intermediate results to a file, which a USS script then processes.

- Example Workflow:
  "JCL writes processed datasets to a temporary file, and a USS script reads the file to generate visualizations."

2. Benefits of Integration:
   - Streamline workflows by combining the strengths of JCL and USS.
   - Leverage familiar tools while introducing modern automation capabilities.
   - Improve flexibility and adaptability for evolving business needs.

By bridging USS and JCL workflows, you'll create hybrid solutions that enhance productivity and drive innovation.

Leveraging Python and Shell Scripts for Enhanced Automation

Python and shell scripts are powerful tools for enhancing automation within USS. These scripting languages allow you to build dynamic, reusable solutions that go beyond the capabilities of traditional mainframe tools.

1. Using Shell Scripts for Task Automation:
   Shell scripts are ideal for automating repetitive tasks, such as file transfers, dataset processing, and log analysis. They provide a lightweight, efficient way to execute commands sequentially or conditionally.
   - Example Script:

```
#!/bin/sh

cp /u/user/input/*.dat /u/user/archive/

echo "Files archived successfully."
```

This script copies all **.dat** files from the input directory to the archive directory.

1. Introducing Python for Advanced Automation:
   Python offers greater flexibility and functionality compared to shell scripts, making it ideal for complex tasks like data analysis, API integrations, and error handling.
   - Example Python Script:

```
import os

for filename in os.listdir("/u/user/input"):

if filename.endswith(".dat"):

os.rename(f"/u/user/input/{filename}", f"/u/user/archive/{filename}")

print("Files moved successfully.")
```

This script moves **.dat** files from the input directory to the archive directory using Python.

1. Combining Python and Shell Scripts:
   You can combine Python and shell scripts to leverage the strengths of both. For example, use a shell script to invoke a Python script for specific tasks.
   - Example Workflow:

```
#!/bin/sh
python3 /u/user/scripts/process_logs.py
echo "Log processing complete."
```

1. Real-World Applications:

- Automating regulatory reporting with Python scripts that analyze datasets and generate compliance reports.
- Using shell scripts to streamline nightly batch jobs while incorporating Python for advanced data transformations.

By leveraging Python and shell scripts, you'll unlock new levels of automation and efficiency within USS.

Cross-Platform Integration with Cloud Environments

As organizations increasingly adopt hybrid IT environments, integrating USS with cloud platforms is becoming a critical capability. Cross-platform integration enables you to bridge the gap between mainframe and cloud systems, unlocking new opportunities for scalability, flexibility, and innovation.

1. Enabling Hybrid Workflows:
   USS can serve as a bridge between mainframe and cloud environments, enabling seamless data exchange and workflow automation. For example, you can use USS scripts to transfer files to cloud storage or invoke cloud-based APIs.
   - Example Use Case:
     "A retail company uses USS scripts to upload inventory data to a cloud-based analytics platform, enabling real-time decision-making."
2. Transferring Files to Cloud Storage:
   Tools like **scp** or **rsync** can be used to transfer files between USS and cloud storage services (e.g., AWS S3, Azure Blob Storage).
   - Example Command:

```
scp /u/user/data/inventory.csv
user@cloudserver:/data/
```

This command uploads a file (**inventory.csv**) to a cloud server.

1. Invoking Cloud APIs from USS:
   Python scripts can be used to interact with cloud APIs, enabling advanced integrations. For example, you can use Python to send data to a cloud-based machine learning model for analysis.
   - Example Python Script:

```
import requests
url = "https://api.cloudservice.com/analyze "
payload = {"data": "processed_data"}
response = requests.post(url, json=payload)
print(response.json())
```

This script sends data to a cloud API for processing.

1. Ensuring Security and Compliance:
   When integrating USS with cloud environments, ensure secure data transfer and access control. Use encryption protocols (e.g., SSH, HTTPS) and follow best practices for managing credentials.
   - Example Security Measure:
     "Use SSH keys for secure file transfers and store API credentials in encrypted files."
2. Real-World Benefits:
   - Enable faster decision-making by integrating mainframe data with cloud-based analytics tools.
   - Support global expansion by leveraging cloud scalability and flexibility.
   - Reduce costs by offloading non-critical workloads to the cloud.

By enabling cross-platform integration, you'll position USS as a key enabler of hybrid IT strategies, driving innovation and efficiency across your organization.

Why Integration Matters

Integrating USS with other technologies is essential for maximizing its value and ensuring alignment with modern IT practices. By bridging USS with JCL workflows, leveraging Python and shell scripts for enhanced automation, and enabling cross-platform integration with cloud environments, you'll create flexible, scalable solutions that meet the demands of today's dynamic business landscape.

With these advanced integration techniques in hand, you're now ready to optimize USS for performance and address security considerations. Let's continue building momentum for USS—one integration at a time.

Chapter 13. Optimizing USS for Performance

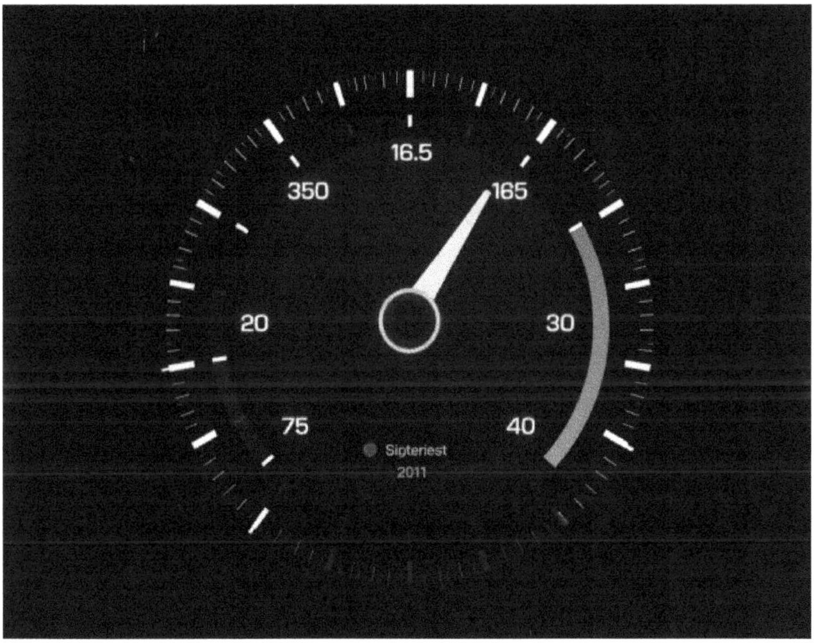

Optimizing z/OS UNIX System Services (USS) for performance is a critical step in ensuring that your workflows run efficiently, reliably, and cost-effectively. In this chapter, we'll explore strategies for reducing resource utilization, improving script efficiency, and avoiding common pitfalls that can hinder performance. By mastering these techniques, you'll create solutions that not only meet business needs but also scale seamlessly as demands grow.

Reducing Resource Utilization

Efficient resource management is essential for maximizing the performance of USS workflows. By reducing CPU, memory, and disk usage, you can free up resources for other tasks and improve overall system throughput.

1. Monitor Resource Usage:
   Use system monitoring tools to track CPU, memory, and disk usage during task execution. Identify bottlenecks and areas for improvement.
    - Example Tools:
        - **top** or **htop** for real-time CPU and memory monitoring.
        - **df** and **du** for analyzing disk space usage.
2. Optimize File Operations:
   Minimize file read/write operations, which can be resource-intensive. For example, avoid repeatedly reading the same file by caching its contents in memory.
    - Example Optimization:
      "Instead of reading a configuration file multiple times, load it into a variable at the start of the script."
3. Use Efficient Data Formats:
   Choose data formats that reduce processing overhead. For example, use compressed files (e.g., **.gz**) for large datasets to save disk space and improve transfer speeds.
    - Example Command:

gzip /u/user/data/largefile.txt
This compresses **largefile.txt**, reducing its size and speeding up transfers.

1. Limit Background Processes:
   Avoid running unnecessary background processes that consume resources. Use tools like **ps** to identify and

terminate unused processes.

- Example Command:

```
ps -ef | grep "unused_process"

kill <PID>
```

By reducing resource utilization, you'll ensure that your USS workflows remain efficient and scalable.

Improving Script Efficiency

Scripts are the backbone of USS automation, but poorly written scripts can lead to inefficiencies. Follow these best practices to write efficient, high-performing scripts.

1. Minimize Redundant Operations:
   Avoid repeating operations unnecessarily. For example, if a calculation or file operation is used multiple times, perform it once and store the result in a variable.
   - Example Optimization:

```
COUNT=$(wc -l < /u/user/data/file.txt)
echo "Line count: $COUNT"
```

This avoids recalculating the line count multiple times.

1. Use Built-In Commands When Possible:
   Built-in commands are often faster and more efficient than external utilities. For example, use shell string manipulation instead of calling **awk** or **sed**.
   - Example Built-In Command:

```
FILENAME="data_backup.tar.gz"
EXTENSION="${FILENAME##*.}"
```

echo "Extension: $EXTENSION"

1. Leverage Parallel Processing:
   Break large tasks into smaller chunks and process them in parallel to reduce execution time. For example, split a dataset into parts and process each part simultaneously.
   - Example Parallel Processing:

split -l 1000 largefile.txt part_

for PART in part_*; do

process_script.sh $PART &

done

wait

This splits **largefile.txt** into smaller files and processes them concurrently.

1. Avoid Unnecessary Logging:
   Excessive logging can slow down scripts and consume disk space. Log only critical information and use log rotation to manage log file sizes.
   - Example Log Rotation:

find /u/user/logs -type f -mtime +7 -exec rm {} \;
This deletes log files older than 7 days.

By writing efficient scripts, you'll ensure that your USS workflows run faster and with fewer errors.

Avoiding Common Pitfalls

Even experienced users can encounter pitfalls when working with USS. Being aware of these challenges and proactively addressing them will help you avoid costly mistakes.

1. Overloading the System:
   Running too many tasks simultaneously can overwhelm system resources. Use scheduling tools like **cron** or workload managers to stagger tasks and balance the load.
   - Example Scheduling:

0 2 * * * /u/user/scripts/nightly_backup.sh

This schedules a nightly backup script to run at 2:00 AM, avoiding peak usage times.

1. Ignoring Error Handling:
   Failing to handle errors can lead to incomplete tasks or corrupted data. Always include error handling in your scripts to detect and address issues.
   - Example Error Handling:

cp /u/user/source/file.txt /u/user/destination/ || echo "Copy failed" >&2

This logs an error message if the copy operation fails.

1. Hardcoding Paths and Values:
   Hardcoding paths or values makes scripts inflexible and prone to errors. Use variables or configuration files instead.
   - Example Variable Usage:

SOURCE_DIR="/u/user/source"
DEST_DIR="/u/user/destination"
cp $SOURCE_DIR/file.txt $DEST_DIR/

1. Neglecting Testing:
   Skipping testing can lead to unexpected failures in production. Test scripts thoroughly in a controlled environment before deploying them.
   - Example Testing Workflow:
     "Run the script on a small dataset to verify functionality before scaling to larger datasets."

By avoiding these common pitfalls, you'll ensure that your USS implementations are robust, reliable, and ready for real-world use.

Why Optimization Matters

Optimizing USS for performance is not just about improving speed—it's about creating scalable, efficient solutions that deliver consistent value. By reducing resource utilization, improving script efficiency, and avoiding common pitfalls, you'll position USS as a cornerstone of your organization's modernization strategy.

With these optimization techniques in hand, you're now ready to address security considerations and ensure that your USS implementations are both secure and compliant. Let's continue building momentum for USS—one optimization at a time.

Chapter 14. Security Considerations in USS

Security is a cornerstone of any IT environment, and z/OS UNIX System Services (USS) is no exception. In this chapter, we'll explore best practices for managing file and directory permissions, protecting sensitive data, and ensuring compliance through auditing. By mastering these security considerations, you'll safeguard your USS implementations against unauthorized access, data breaches, and compliance violations.

Best Practices for File and Directory Permissions

Properly managing file and directory permissions is essential for maintaining the integrity and security of your USS environment. Misconfigured permissions can lead to unauthorized access or accidental modifications, compromising sensitive data.

1. Understanding Permissions:
   Permissions in USS are divided into three categories:
   - Read (**r**): Allows viewing the contents of a file or listing directory contents.
   - Write (**w**): Allows modifying or deleting a file or adding/removing files in a directory.
   - Execute (**x**): Allows running a file as a script or accessing files within a directory.

These permissions apply to three groups:

- Owner: The user who owns the file or directory.
- Group: Users who belong to the file's group.
- Others: All other users.

1. Setting Permissions with **chmod**:
   Use the **chmod** command to set or modify permissions. For example:

chmod 750 sensitive_file.txt
This sets the following permissions:

- Owner: Read, write, and execute (**7**).
- Group: Read and execute (**5**).
- Others: No permissions (**0**).

1. Changing Ownership with **chown**:
   Use the **chown** command to change the owner or group of a

file or directory. For example:

chown admin:finance sensitive_file.txt
This assigns ownership to the user **admin** and the group **finance**.

1. Restricting Access to Sensitive Files:
   Limit access to sensitive files by applying strict permissions. For example:

chmod 600 confidential_data.txt
This ensures that only the owner can read and write the file.

1. Using Sticky Bits for Shared Directories:
   For shared directories, use the sticky bit to ensure that only the file owner can delete or rename their own files. For example:

chmod +t /u/user/shared/

By implementing these best practices, you'll ensure that your file and directory permissions align with the principle of least privilege, minimizing the risk of unauthorized access.

Protecting Sensitive Data

Sensitive data, such as personally identifiable information (PII), financial records, or intellectual property, requires special attention to prevent exposure or misuse. Here's how to protect sensitive data in USS:

1. Encrypting Data at Rest:
   Use encryption tools to protect sensitive files stored on disk. For example, use GNU Privacy Guard (GPG) to encrypt files:

gpg -c sensitive_file.txt
This creates an encrypted version of the file (**sensitive_file.txt.gpg**).

1. Securing Data in Transit:
   When transferring sensitive data, use secure protocols like SSH or HTTPS to prevent interception. For example:

scp sensitive_file.txt user@secure_server:/data/
This securely copies the file to a remote server using SSH.

1. Masking Sensitive Information in Logs:
   Avoid logging sensitive data, such as passwords or credit card numbers. If logging is necessary, mask sensitive fields before writing them to logs.
   - Example Masking Script:

```
sed
's/[0-9]\{4\}-[0-9]\{4\}-[0-9]\{4\}-[0-9]\{4\}/XXXX-XXXX-X
g' input.log > masked.log
```

This replaces credit card numbers in a log file with XXXX-XXXX-XXXX-XXXX.

1. Implementing Role-Based Access Control (RBAC):
   Restrict access to sensitive data based on user roles. For example, grant access only to users who require it for their job functions.
2. Using Secure Storage Locations:
   Store sensitive data in dedicated, restricted directories with minimal access. For example:

mkdir /u/user/secure_data

chmod 700 /u/user/secure_data
This creates a secure directory accessible only by the owner.

By protecting sensitive data, you'll reduce the risk of data breaches and ensure compliance with privacy regulations.

Auditing and Compliance

Auditing and compliance are critical components of a secure USS environment. Regular audits help identify vulnerabilities, enforce policies, and demonstrate adherence to regulatory requirements.

1. Enabling Auditing Features:
   Use USS auditing tools to track access and modifications to files and directories. For example, configure audit logs to record specific events:
    - File access attempts.
    - Permission changes.
    - Script executions.
    - Example Audit Log Configuration:
      "Enable logging for all file modifications in /**u**/**user**/**sensitive**/."
2. Reviewing Logs Regularly:
   Regularly review audit logs to detect unusual activity or policy violations. Use tools like **grep** and **awk** to filter and analyze logs.
    - Example Log Analysis:

grep "ERROR" /u/user/logs/audit.log
This identifies error messages in the audit log.

1. Conducting Periodic Security Assessments:
   Perform regular assessments to evaluate the security of your USS environment. Include checks for:
    - Proper file and directory permissions.

    - Encryption of sensitive data.
    - Compliance with organizational policies and regulations.
2. Ensuring Regulatory Compliance:
   Align your USS implementations with industry standards and regulations, such as GDPR, HIPAA, or PCI DSS. For example:
    - Encrypt PII to comply with GDPR.
    - Restrict access to healthcare records to comply with HIPAA.
3. Documenting Security Policies:
   Maintain clear documentation of your security policies and procedures. This ensures consistency and provides a reference for audits and compliance reviews.

By implementing robust auditing and compliance practices, you'll build trust with stakeholders and demonstrate your commitment to security.

Why Security Matters

Security is not just a technical requirement—it's a business imperative. By following best practices for file and directory permissions, protecting sensitive data, and ensuring compliance through auditing, you'll create a secure USS environment that safeguards your organization's assets and reputation.

With these security considerations in hand, you've now completed your journey through "Mastering USS Made Simple: A Practical Guide to Modernizing Your Mainframe Without Linux Expertise." You're equipped with the knowledge and skills to leverage USS effectively, drive modernization initiatives, and position yourself as a leader in mainframe innovation. Congratulations on achieving this milestone, and remember: the journey to mastery is ongoing. Keep learning, experimenting, and pushing the boundaries of what's possible with USS!

Let's continue building a future where mainframes remain a powerful, modern asset—one secure, optimized workflow at a time.

Conclusion

Welcome to the Conclusion , where we bring together everything you've learned and prepare you for the next steps in your journey with z/OS UNIX System Services (USS). This final section serves as both a reflection on your progress and a launchpad for future growth. Whether you're just beginning to apply USS in real-world scenarios or looking to deepen your expertise, these chapters will guide you in consolidating your knowledge and continuing your exploration of mainframe modernization.

Why Focus on the Conclusion?

The conclusion is more than a summary—it's an opportunity to reinforce the skills and insights you've gained throughout this book. It's also a chance to think critically about how to apply what you've learned in practical, impactful ways. Additionally, it provides resources and guidance to help you stay current, connected, and inspired as you advance in your career.

What You'll Learn in This Part

This section is divided into two key chapters, each designed to support your ongoing success:

1. Putting It All Together: Your Path to Mastery
   In this chapter, we'll recap the key takeaways from the book, reflect on how to apply them in real-world situations, and discuss strategies for continuing your journey in mainframe modernization. This chapter will leave you with a clear roadmap for leveraging USS effectively and confidently.

2. Additional Resources
   No learning journey ends with a single book. This chapter highlights recommended reading, online courses, tools, utilities, and communities that will help you expand your knowledge and connect with others in the field. These resources are invaluable for staying ahead in the ever-evolving world of mainframe technology.

How This Part Fits Into the Bigger Picture

The conclusion ties together all the threads of your learning experience, ensuring that you leave this book not only with theoretical knowledge but also with actionable insights and practical tools. By reflecting on key takeaways, applying your skills, and exploring additional resources, you'll be well-prepared to tackle modernization challenges and continue growing as a leader in the field.

By the end of this part, you'll have a comprehensive understanding of how to put your USS expertise into practice and a clear plan for advancing your skills further. Let's wrap up this journey by celebrating your achievements and preparing you for the exciting opportunities ahead.

Let's dive in and explore how to turn your newfound knowledge into lasting impact—one step at a time.

Chapter 15. Putting It All Together: Your Path to Mastery

Congratulations on reaching this pivotal moment in your journey with z/OS UNIX System Services (USS)! You've learned the foundational skills, explored advanced techniques, and gained insights into best practices for modernizing your mainframe environment. Now it's time to consolidate your knowledge, reflect on how to apply what you've learned, and chart a course for continued growth. In this chapter, we'll recap the key takeaways, discuss real-world applications, and outline strategies for advancing your expertise in mainframe modernization.

Recap of Key Takeaways

Throughout this book, you've acquired a wealth of knowledge that positions you as a capable and confident USS practitioner. Let's revisit the core lessons that will serve as the foundation of your success:

1. Foundations of USS:
    - Mastered essential commands for navigation, file management, and permissions (**cd**, **ls**, **chmod**, etc.).
    - Learned how to automate tasks with shell scripts, leveraging variables, loops, and conditionals.
    - Gained proficiency in monitoring workflows and troubleshooting issues using logs, **tail -f**, **grep**, and **awk**.
2. Aligning USS with Business Goals:
    - Connected USS capabilities to organizational objectives like cost reduction, efficiency improvement, and scalability.
    - Drafted compelling modernization proposals and communicated the value of USS to stakeholders.
    - Demonstrated measurable results through KPIs like task completion rates, error reductions, and resource utilization.
3. Executing and Scaling USS Initiatives:
    - Planned and implemented pilot projects to test feasibility and gather actionable feedback.
    - Scaled USS solutions across teams while managing change and overcoming resistance.
    - Ensured long-term success through continuous monitoring, optimization, and stakeholder engagement.

4. Advanced Topics and Best Practices:
    - Integrated USS with other technologies, such as JCL workflows, Python, and cloud environments.
    - Optimized USS for performance by reducing resource utilization and improving script efficiency.
    - Addressed security considerations, including file permissions, data protection, and auditing.

These takeaways form the backbone of your USS expertise, equipping you to tackle modernization challenges with confidence and creativity.

Applying What You've Learned in the Real World

The true measure of mastery lies in applying your knowledge to solve real-world problems. Here's how you can put your skills into practice and drive meaningful impact within your organization:

1. Start Small, Think Big:
   Begin by identifying a specific process or workflow that can benefit from USS automation. For example:
    - Automate nightly batch jobs to reduce manual effort and errors.
    - Streamline file transfers between mainframe and cloud environments.
    - Use Python scripts to analyze datasets and generate actionable insights.
2. Measure and Demonstrate Value:
   Track KPIs to quantify the impact of your initiatives. For instance:
    - Reduced processing times by 30%.
    - Eliminated manual errors, improving accuracy by 80%.
    - Saved $50,000 annually in labor costs through

automation.
Share these metrics with leadership to build trust and secure resources for broader adoption.

3. Collaborate Across Teams:
   Engage colleagues from IT, operations, and business units to ensure your solutions meet diverse needs. For example:
   - Work with the finance team to automate regulatory reporting.
   - Partner with developers to integrate USS with cloud-based analytics tools.
   - Train end users to adopt new workflows seamlessly.
4. Iterate and Improve:
   Modernization is an ongoing process. Continuously refine your solutions based on feedback and evolving requirements. For example:
   - Optimize scripts to reduce CPU usage.
   - Add error notifications to improve transparency.
   - Expand automation to additional workflows as demand grows.

By applying your skills thoughtfully and strategically, you'll position USS as a transformative tool that drives efficiency, innovation, and value across your organization.

Continuing Your Journey in Mainframe Modernization

Your journey with USS doesn't end here—it's just the beginning. Mainframe modernization is a dynamic field, and staying ahead requires continuous learning, experimentation, and collaboration. Here are some strategies to help you continue growing:

1. Stay Current with Industry Trends:
   The world of technology is constantly evolving. Keep up with the latest developments in USS, mainframe modernization,

and hybrid IT environments by reading blogs, attending webinars, and following industry leaders.

2. Expand Your Skill Set:
   Build on your USS expertise by exploring related technologies, such as:
   - Advanced scripting languages (e.g., Python, Perl).
   - Cloud platforms (e.g., AWS, Azure, Google Cloud).
   - DevOps practices and CI/CD pipelines.
3. Engage with Communities:
   Join forums, user groups, and professional organizations to connect with peers and share knowledge. For example:
   - Participate in IBM Z and USS-focused communities.
   - Attend conferences like SHARE or IBM TechU to learn from experts.
   - Contribute to open-source projects or mentor others in the field.
4. Pursue Certifications and Training:
   Formal certifications and courses can deepen your expertise and enhance your credibility. Consider pursuing certifications in:
   - IBM Z and USS technologies.
   - Cloud computing and hybrid IT solutions.
   - Cybersecurity and compliance frameworks.
5. Experiment and Innovate:
   Don't be afraid to push boundaries and try new approaches. Experiment with integrating USS into emerging use cases, such as AI-driven analytics, IoT data processing, or blockchain-enabled workflows.

By embracing lifelong learning and staying curious, you'll remain at the forefront of mainframe modernization and continue to drive innovation in your organization.

Why Mastery Matters

Mastery of USS is not just about technical proficiency—it's about creating value, solving problems, and leading change. By mastering USS, you've positioned yourself as a catalyst for modernization, capable of bridging the gap between legacy systems and future innovations. Whether you're automating workflows, securing sensitive data, or scaling solutions across teams, your contributions will have a lasting impact on your organization's success.

As you move forward, remember that mastery is a journey, not a destination. Keep applying what you've learned, stay connected to the community, and never stop exploring new possibilities. With your newfound expertise, you're ready to transform your mainframe environment and shape the future of IT.

Congratulations once again on completing this journey. The path to mastery is challenging, but the rewards are immense. Let's continue building a future where mainframes remain a powerful, modern asset—one innovative solution at a time.

Onward and upward!

Chapter 16. Additional Resources

Your journey with z/OS UNIX System Services (USS) doesn't end here—there's always more to learn, explore, and achieve. To help you continue growing as a USS practitioner and mainframe modernization expert, we've compiled a list of recommended resources, tools, and communities. These resources will deepen your knowledge, enhance your skills, and connect you with like-minded professionals who share your passion for innovation.

Recommended Reading and Online Courses

Staying informed and expanding your expertise requires access to high-quality learning materials. Here are some books, articles, and online courses to guide your continued education:

1. Books:
    - *"z/OS UNIX System Services: A Practical Guide"* by IBM Redbooks
      This comprehensive guide provides in-depth insights into USS concepts, commands, and best practices.
    - *"Mastering the Mainframe: Modern Techniques for z/OS"* by John E. Swanson
      A practical resource for modernizing mainframe environments, including USS integration and automation.
    - *"UNIX and Linux System Administration Handbook"* by Evi Nemeth et al.
      While not specific to USS, this classic book covers UNIX/Linux system administration principles that align closely with USS workflows.
2. Articles and Whitepapers:
    - IBM Developer Tutorials: Explore tutorials on USS scripting, automation, and cloud integration at IBM Developer (https://developer.ibm.com/)[1].
    - Gartner Reports: Stay updated on mainframe modernization trends and strategies through industry-leading research.
3. Online Courses:
    - Coursera:
        - *"Mainframe Modernization with IBM Z"* – Learn how to leverage USS and other technologies for modernization.

1. https://developer.ibm.com/

        - *"Introduction to Shell Scripting"* – Master scripting techniques applicable to USS workflows.
    - Udemy:
        - *"Automating Tasks with Shell Scripts"* – Build advanced scripting skills for USS automation.
        - *"Cloud Computing for Mainframe Professionals"* – Explore hybrid IT strategies and cloud integration.
    - IBM Training:
      IBM offers specialized courses on USS, JCL, and z/OS through its training portal. Visit IBM Training (https://www.ibm.com/training)[2] for details.

By leveraging these resources, you'll stay ahead of the curve and deepen your understanding of USS and related technologies.

Tools and Utilities for USS Development

The right tools can make all the difference in streamlining your USS workflows and enhancing productivity. Here are some essential tools and utilities to support your development efforts:

1. Text Editors and IDEs:
    - vi/vim: A lightweight, powerful text editor available in USS for creating and editing scripts.
    - nano: A user-friendly text editor ideal for beginners.
    - Visual Studio Code (VS Code): Use the Remote SSH extension to edit USS files directly from your local machine.
2. Scripting Tools:
    - Bash: The default shell for USS, perfect for writing and executing scripts.
    - Python: Use Python for advanced automation, data analysis, and API integrations.

---

2. https://www.ibm.com/training

    - Perl: A versatile scripting language for text processing and complex workflows.
3. Monitoring and Debugging Tools:
    - tail -f: Monitor log files in real-time to track task progress and identify issues.
    - grep and awk: Extract insights from logs and analyze data efficiently.
    - strace: Trace system calls and signals to debug scripts and diagnose performance bottlenecks.
4. File Transfer Utilities:
    - scp: Securely transfer files between USS and remote servers.
    - rsync: Synchronize files and directories across systems with minimal bandwidth usage.
    - FTP/SFTP: Use secure file transfer protocols for cross-platform data exchange.
5. Encryption and Security Tools:
    - GPG (GNU Privacy Guard): Encrypt sensitive files to protect data at rest.
    - OpenSSL: Generate certificates and encrypt data in transit.
    - chmod and chown: Manage file and directory permissions effectively.

By incorporating these tools into your workflow, you'll streamline development, improve efficiency, and ensure robust security.

Communities and Forums for Support

No one masters USS alone—communities and forums provide invaluable opportunities to learn, collaborate, and troubleshoot challenges. Here are some vibrant communities where you can connect with fellow USS practitioners:

1. IBM Communities:
    - IBM Z and USS User Groups: Join regional or virtual user groups to share experiences and best practices.
    - IBM Developer Community: Engage with developers and experts on the IBM Developer Forums (https://community.ibm.com/community/user/developer)[3].
2. Professional Organizations:
    - SHARE: A leading organization for mainframe professionals, offering conferences, workshops, and networking opportunities. Visit SHARE (https://www.share.org/)[4] to get involved.
    - CMG (Computer Measurement Group): Focuses on performance, capacity planning, and modernization strategies.
3. Online Forums and Discussion Boards:
    - Stack Overflow: Search for USS-related questions or post your own queries to get answers from the global developer community.
    - Reddit: Subreddits like r/mainframe and r/sysadmin are great places to discuss USS challenges and innovations.
    - LinkedIn Groups: Join groups like "Mainframe Modernization" or "z/OS Professionals" to network with industry leaders.
4. Conferences and Events:
    - IBM TechU: An annual event featuring hands-on labs, sessions, and networking opportunities focused on USS and z/OS technologies.

---

3. https://community.ibm.com/community/user/developer

4. https://www.share.org/

- GSE Nordic Conference: Explores mainframe modernization trends, including USS integration and automation.

By engaging with these communities, you'll gain access to a wealth of knowledge, mentorship, and collaboration opportunities that will accelerate your growth as a USS expert.

Why Additional Resources Matter

The field of mainframe modernization is constantly evolving, and staying ahead requires a commitment to lifelong learning. By leveraging recommended reading, tools, and communities, you'll build a strong foundation for continued success. These resources will not only enhance your technical skills but also connect you with a global network of professionals who share your passion for innovation.

As you continue your journey, remember that every challenge is an opportunity to grow, and every connection is a chance to learn. With these resources at your fingertips, you're well-equipped to tackle new challenges, drive meaningful change, and position yourself as a leader in the world of USS and mainframe modernization.

Here's to your continued success—keep exploring, experimenting, and innovating. The future of mainframe technology is in your hands!

Epilogue: The Future of USS and Your Role in Shaping It

As we bring this journey to a close, take a moment to reflect on how far you've come. From mastering the foundational commands of z/OS UNIX System Services (USS) to exploring advanced topics like automation, integration, and security, you've acquired the skills and knowledge needed to modernize your mainframe environment effectively. But more importantly, you've gained the confidence to tackle real-world challenges and drive meaningful change within your organization.

The mainframe has long been the backbone of enterprise IT systems, and with technologies like USS, it continues to evolve and adapt to the demands of the digital age. By embracing USS, you're not just preserving the legacy of the mainframe—you're transforming it into a platform for innovation, efficiency, and growth. Whether you're automating workflows, integrating with cloud environments, or securing sensitive data, your contributions are shaping the future of IT.

But the journey doesn't end here. The world of technology is dynamic, and staying ahead requires curiosity, creativity, and collaboration. As new tools, frameworks, and methodologies emerge, you'll have opportunities to push the boundaries of what's possible with USS. Imagine leveraging AI-driven analytics to optimize resource utilization, using blockchain to secure transactions, or integrating IoT data streams into your workflows. The possibilities are endless—and so is your potential to lead.

Your role as a USS practitioner is more than technical—it's transformative. You're not just solving problems; you're creating solutions that empower businesses, enhance customer experiences, and drive strategic outcomes. Every script you write, every workflow you automate, and every stakeholder you inspire brings us closer to a future where mainframes remain a powerful, modern asset.

So, as you step forward into this next chapter of your journey, remember these key principles:

- Stay Curious: Never stop learning. Explore new technologies, experiment with innovative approaches, and challenge yourself to grow.
- Collaborate: Engage with communities, share your knowledge, and learn from others. Together, we can achieve more than any one of us could alone.
- Lead with Purpose: Use your expertise to solve real-world problems and create lasting value. Your work has the power to transform organizations and improve lives.

Thank you for embarking on this journey with me. I hope this book has inspired you to see USS not just as a tool but as a catalyst for change—a way to bridge the past and the future, tradition and innovation, stability and agility.

The future of USS is bright, and it's yours to shape. Go forth with confidence, creativity, and determination. The mainframe world is waiting for leaders like you to take it to new heights.

Here's to your success—and to the limitless possibilities ahead.

Onward and upward!

Don't miss out!

Visit the website below and you can sign up to receive emails whenever Ricardo Nuqui publishes a new book. There's no charge and no obligation.

https://books2read.com/r/B-A-NBRMC-PVGJG

BOOKS 2 READ

Connecting independent readers to independent writers.

Did you love *Mastering USS Made Simple: A Practical Guide to Modernizing Your Mainframe Without Linux Expertise*? Then you should read *Future-Proof z/OS: A Comprehensive Guide to Mainframe Modernization*[1] by Ricardo Nuqui!

[2]

Future-Proof z/OS: A Comprehensive Guide to Mainframe Modernization*Transforming Legacy Systems into Agile, Resilient, and Innovation-Driven Platforms*

In a world where digital transformation is no longer optional, the IBM z/OS mainframe remains a trusted backbone of enterprise IT—celebrated for its reliability, scalability, and security. Yet, as organizations adopt hybrid cloud architectures, AI-driven analytics, and DevOps practices, modernizing these legacy systems has become critical to staying competitive and future-ready. *Future-Proof z/OS: A*

1. https://books2read.com/u/3njW1P

2. https://books2read.com/u/3njW1P

Comprehensive Guide to Mainframe Modernization is your definitive roadmap to transforming traditional mainframes into agile, efficient, and innovation-driven platforms that meet the demands of today and tomorrow.

This book provides a step-by-step exploration of every facet of mainframe modernization. From foundational strategies to advanced techniques, you'll learn how to monitor system health, optimize performance, scale workloads dynamically, and implement predictive maintenance using cutting-edge tools like IBM Watson AIOps, Kubernetes, and Red Hat OpenShift. Packed with real-world case studies, hands-on exercises, and practical insights, this guide bridges the gap between theory and action, empowering you to solve real-world challenges effectively.

What You'll Learn:

Foundations of Modernization: Understand the drivers, challenges, and approaches to modernizing IBM z/OS environments while preserving their strengths.**Monitoring and Optimization:** Harness tools and techniques to improve system performance, reduce resource bottlenecks, and lower operational costs.**Dynamic Scaling and Hybrid Cloud Integration:** Master workload scaling, containerization, and hybrid cloud strategies to ensure seamless adaptability to fluctuating demands.**AI-Driven Operations:** Leverage predictive analytics, anomaly detection, and automation to anticipate issues, prevent downtime, and optimize workflows.**Security and Compliance:** Protect sensitive data, ensure regulatory adherence, and safeguard against modern cybersecurity threats in a rapidly evolving IT landscape.**Practical Applications:** Apply proven strategies from real-world scenarios across industries—including financial institutions, retail companies, and healthcare providers—to achieve measurable outcomes.

Whether you're an IT professional managing legacy systems, a developer integrating modern technologies, or a business leader driving strategic transformation, this book equips you with the skills and knowledge to lead successful modernization initiatives. Written in clear, accessible language and enriched with actionable advice, *Future-Proof z/OS* is your ultimate guide to unlocking the full potential of your mainframe environment.

Transform your z/OS systems into resilient, agile platforms that not only meet current demands but also lay the foundation for innovation and growth in the years to come.

Also by Ricardo Nuqui

CyberSecurity
The CISSP Fast-Track: Conquer the 8 Domains

Mainframes
Mastering Mainframe Modernization
Mainframe Meets Modernization: Mastering Hybrid Cloud Design
Mainframe Mastery with DevOps: Integrating Legacy Systems with Agile Practices
Mainframe Modernization: CI/CD Mastery
Mainframe to Cloud Mastery: Best Practices
Mainframe Modernization with DevOps Mastery
Mainframe Containerization Mastery
Future-Proof Your Mainframes with AI/ML
Smart Architectures: AI/ML in Mainframe-Cloud Environments
Future-Proof z/OS: A Comprehensive Guide to Mainframe Modernization
Mastering USS Made Simple: A Practical Guide to Modernizing Your Mainframe Without Linux Expertise

www.ingramcontent.com/pod-product-compliance
Ingram Content Group UK Ltd.
Pitfield, Milton Keynes, MK11 3LW, UK
UKHW020124290926
15471UKWH00003B/258

9 798231 764044